W9-BWF-780

Building Bridges

Building Bridges

Interreligious Dialogue
on the Path to World Peace

An Interview by Helmut S. Ruppert
with Cardinal Francis Arinze

Foreword by Donald W. Mitchell

New City Press

Published in the United States by New City Press
202 Cardinal Rd., Hyde Park, NY 12538
www.newcitypress.com
©2004 New City Press

Translated by Gene Selzer, with revisions by the author,
from the original German edition *Brücken Bauen*
©2000 Sankt Ulrich Verlag, Augsburg, Germany

Cover design by Miguel Tejerina and Nick Cianfarani

Library of Congress Cataloging-in-Publication Data:
    [Brücken bauen. English]
    Building bridges : interreligious dialogue on the path to world peace : an interview /
      by Helmut S. Ruppert with Francis Arinze ; foreword by Donald W. Mitchell ;
      [translated by Gene Selzer ; with revisions by the author].
         p. cm.
    ISBN 1-56548-203-4
      1. Arinze, Francis A.--Interviews. 2. Theology of religions (Christian theology) 3.
    Christianity and other religions. 4. Catholic Church--Relations. 5. Cardinals--
    Interviews.
      I. Ruppert, Helmut S. II. Title

    BT83.85.B7813 2004
    261.2--dc22   2004049864

Printed in the United States of America

Contents

Foreword

Today, we are living in a new world of religious pluralism. By *pluralism*, I do not mean that there are many religions in the world. There have always been many religions. But today people of different religions are encountering each other in ways that were not possible in the past. Due to new forms of transportation and communication, economic globalization, and more possibilities for immigration, people of various religions find themselves meeting each other, working with each other, and living with each other much more than in the past. These types of everyday encounters, and the blending of different religious communities in the fabric of modern and especially urban societies, has brought about the need for religious people and their communities to reflect on their own religious identity in relation to the religious identities of their neighbors.

This kind of reflection has led to different conclusions. At one extreme, some have concluded, as Cardinal Francis Arinze has pointed out, that all religions are more or less the same. It is argued that they all affirm similar kinds of ethical values and hold similar views. While their religious practices seem outwardly different, they are said to produce similar kinds of experiences, so they are simply different paths to the same summit. Persons holding this conclusion do not see any significant differences between the world's religions, and are indifferent to the claims of uniqueness that any of them might make. This kind of indifference to difference makes religiously committed persons, like Cardinal Arinze, uncomfortable. Arinze points out that these persons are missing the fundamental point of authentic Christian faith: the central and unique role of Jesus Christ in salvation history.

At the other extreme, some persons have concluded that religious differences are so momentous that they simply cannot be tolerated. Cardinal Arinze rightly calls these persons *extremists*. It is not that they are just *fundamentalists*, persons who hold firmly to what they believe are the fundamentals of their faith and try to conserve the traditions and practices that they find essential to their faith life. Extremists reject the value of other religions and define the value of persons of other religions only in terms of their potential to be converted. Sometimes extremists even claim that other religions are the product of an evil force. They then dehumanize persons of other religions and try to deny them even their most basic human rights.

The majority of sincerely religious persons are not on the leftwing or rightwing fringes of their traditions. They maintain a position that affirms the uniqueness and value of their own religious identity while being open to the positive value of other religions. They recognize both the similarities and the differences between their religion and those of their neighbors. True interreligious dialogue, as Cardinal Arinze says, is based on this dual recognition. It does not compromise the uniqueness of what distinguishes one's own dearly-held beliefs, but finds the similarities in views and shared values to be bridges to mutual understanding and respect upon which cooperation can be developed for the good of all persons in a community, nation or the world.

If we look at Christianity, we find a spectrum of viewpoints concerning the validity and value of other religions. It is important to note that these viewpoints in turn determine the openness of a Christian to interreligious dialogue. At one end of the spectrum is the "pluralist" viewpoint that sees Christianity as just one way among many that God has revealed God's reality and will to humankind. Jesus Christ is said to be one savior among many through whom God brings people to salvation. An important concern about the pluralistic point of view is that it can lead to indifferentism or syncretism by compromising certain fundamental Christian teachings about the centrality of Christ in the history of salvation.

At the other end of the spectrum is the "exclusivist" viewpoint that sees Christianity as the only true faith, as the exclusive revelation of God's reality and will, and the only way to salvation. Since Jesus Christ is the only savior of humanity, the argument goes, it is only through a conscious acceptance of him as one's personal savior that one can be saved. From this viewpoint, all the rest of humankind are lost souls and their religions cannot give them any access to salvation. An important concern with this point of view is that while it does put Jesus Christ at the center of salvation history, the circle of his saving grace is too small. It denies that Christ can bring grace into the lives of persons of other religions as well as their religious traditions and cultures. Such a view can lead to religious extremism, intolerance and fanaticism.

Between these two ends of the spectrum lies a third viewpoint, the "inclusivist" perspective. The inclusivist claim is that God's full and definitive revelation is in and through Jesus Christ, who is the one source of salvation. What separates the inclusivist from the exclusivist is that the former also claims that the grace of God in Jesus Christ is not limited to the baptized Christian community. God's saving grace extends through Christ into the lives, traditions and cultures of persons of other religions. If those persons follow the truths and will of God revealed to their conscience, even if they do not know its ultimate source, they can find salvation.

This more moderate viewpoint balances a traditional affirmation of the uniqueness of Christ and the centrality of the paschal mystery in salvation history, with an openness to God's grace at work in the lives, traditions and cultures of all religious peoples. It is this more moderate and balanced point of view that the Catholic Church embraces. Therefore on the one hand the Church gives witness to Christ, and on the other hand engages in interreligious dialogue with persons of other religions. Proclamation shares with the world the gospel message. Dialogue enters into a mutual sharing of life, theology, spirituality and cooperation in order to foster greater mutual understanding and appreciation of God's work in the lives of religious persons and in the traditions and cultures of the world's religions.

One basis for the Catholic Church's positive dialogue with other religions is the following statement in *Nostra aetate*:

Men look to their different religions for an answer
to the unsolved riddles of human existence . . .
throughout history even to the present day, there
is found among different peoples a certain awareness of a hidden power, which lies behind the
course of nature and the events of human life. . . .
The Catholic Church rejects nothing of what is
true and holy in these religions. She has high
regard for the manner of life and conduct, the
precepts and doctrines which, although differing
in many ways from her own teachings, nevertheless often reflect a ray of that truth which
enlightens all men. (#1, 2)

Building on this view of other religions, Pope Paul VI
said, "The Church respects and esteems [other religions]
because...they carry within them the echo of thousands
of years of searching for God. . . . They are all impregnated
with the innumerable seeds of the Word" (*Evangelii
nuntiandi*, #53).

One of the goals of interfaith dialogue is, then, to
discover these rays or seeds of the Word. As Pope John
Paul II says in *Redemptoris missio*:

Through dialogue, the Church seeks to uncover
the seeds of the Word . . . those found in individuals and in the religious traditions of mankind. . . .
[Other religions] stimulate [the Church] both to
discover and acknowledge the signs of Christ's
presence and of the working of the Spirit, as well
as to examine more deeply her own identity and to
bear witness to the fullness of Revelation which
she has received for the good of all. (#55-56)

I would add here that in this same document John Paul II says that "God does not fail to make himself present in many ways, not only to individuals but also to entire peoples through their spiritual riches, of which their religions are the main and essential expression" (#55). Here, the Church explicitly states that it respects other religions because they are a means by which God has communicated with humankind.

As for the question concerning the possibility of persons of other religions attaining salvation, Cardinal Walter Kasper summarizes *Lumen gentium,* #16, in this way:

> The council confirmed the theological teaching that God, who is the salvation of all human beings . . . shows the way to salvation to those who, through no fault of their own, do not know Jesus Christ but, moved by grace, try in their actions to do God's will as they know it through the dictates of their conscience. (*Pro dialogo*, 2001/1, p. 82)

Kasper goes on to say that Vatican II rejected any view that claims that those who do not acknowledge the Christian faith are forever lost:

> [Vatican II] attempts to explain on the basis of the teaching of the Scripture and the fathers of the Church that in Jesus Christ salvation has come to all people in a universal way that includes everything that is true and good in the other religions. That means that salvation, which non-Christians can share in if they live according to their conscience, is not some other type of salvation

outside of and without Jesus Christ, but more of a salvation in and through Jesus Christ. (*Ibid.*, p. 84)

This is a clear statement of the Catholic Church's teaching concerning Christ's grace at work outside the visible church in ways that bring persons of other faiths into the paschal mystery of salvation. As Pope John Paul II says in *Redemptoris missio*, the Spirit of God brings each person the possibility "of sharing in the paschal mystery in a manner known to God. . . . The Spirit's presence and activity affect not only the individuals, but also society and history, peoples, cultures and religions" (#28). About this work of the Holy Spirit in other religions, Pope John Paul II also says, "we can maintain that every authentic prayer is called forth by the Holy Spirit, who is mysteriously present in the hearts of every person" (*Address to the Cardinals and Roman Curia*, 22 December 1986).

The Vatican's Congregation for the Doctrine of the Faith clearly states in *Dominus Iesus*, #20, that the work of the Holy Spirit in the hearts of all people brings salvation to persons of other religions.

For those who are not formally and visibly members of the church, "salvation in Christ is accessible by virtue of a grace which, while having a mysterious relationship to the church, does not make them formally part of the church but enlightens them in a way which is accommodated to their spiritual and material situation. This grace comes from Christ; it is the result of his sacrifice and is communicated by the Holy Spirit" (quoting *Redemptoris missio*, #10).

In this statement, both the Congregation and the pope are affirming the inclusivist position concerning salvation of persons of other religions.

Based on this inclusivist openness to dialogue with other relgions, the dialogical experience of the Catholic Church has taught that there are fundamentally four types of inter-religious dialogue discussed by Cardinal Arinze. First is the dialogue of life. Given that we live in a pluralistic society, we find ourselves interacting with persons of different religions. This daily contact with people of other faiths becomes the context for the dialogue of life. It is the grass-roots lived experience of building interfaith friendships, sharing one's faith and learning about the faith of others, in ways that build mutual understanding, respect and enrichment between people and their religious communities. This form of dialogue has been a strength of the Focolare, publisher of this book, with Buddhists and Hindus in Asia, Jews in Europe, South America, Israel and the United States, and Muslims in North Africa, the Middle East, South Asia and the United States.

Second is the dialogue of action or collaboration. Here persons of different religions, or groups or organizations work together to address issues of injustice, poverty, or other social or environmental issues that are of mutual concern. The intention here is also to sow seeds of peace and unity in our world through interfaith cooperation. One is reminded of the World Day of Prayer for Peace in Assisi in 1986, or the more recent day of prayer for peace in Assisi in 2002, attended by world religious leaders invited by the pope in response to the events of 11 September 2001. There, leaders of all faiths addressed together the evil of terrorism.

Third is the dialogue of experts, or the theological dialogue that seeks to uncover the similarities and differences between our religious tradition and those of other religions. Here, among other things, theologians search for the rays or seeds of the Word in other religions, as well as try to discern how it is that persons of other faiths participate in the paschal mystery of redemption, the source of salvation. As it says in *Dominus Iesus*: "Theologians are seeking to understand this question more fully. Their work is to be encouraged, since it is certainly useful for understanding better God's salvific plan and the ways in which it is accomplished" (#21).

Fourth is the dialogue on the spiritual life that seeks to explore together the practice of prayer and meditation, and the spirituality and experience of the religions of the world. In this kind of encounter, one is probing the contemplative core of religious life as it is expressed in various religions. In this regard, the Church has been especially interested in dialogue with Asian religions. The Benedictine tradition has established the Monastic Inter-religious Dialogue to carry out intermonastic exchanges and dialogues with both Buddhists and Hindus. This work has resulted in the 1996 and 2003 Gethsemani Encounters between Christian and Buddhist monastic leaders, including His Holiness the Dalai Lama, from around the world. They meet together at Gethsemani Abbey, home of Thomas Merton, to discuss the spiritual life and its relevance for humankind today.

For almost 20 years, Cardinal Francis Arinze has been at the forefront of the Catholic Church's initiatives in the field of interreligious dialogue. Born in Nigeria in 1932 to parents who practiced an African indigenous religion,

Arinze converted to Christianity at the age of nine. He was ordained a priest in 1958, and was named bishop in 1965 and archbishop of Ontisha in 1967. In 1984, Pope John Paul II chose him to be president of the Vatican's Pontifical Council for Interreligious Dialogue, where he served until 2002. In 1985, Arinze was made a cardinal. In his capacity at the Pontifical Council for Interreligious Dialogue, Cardinal Arinze tirelessly traveled the globe in pursuing greater interfaith understanding and appreciation between the Catholic Church and other religions. Publishing this book at this time is certainly a fitting recognition of Cardinal Arinze's extraordinary work in the field of interreligious dialogue and the historic contributions he has made in that field for so many years.

Given the political, economic, social and ethnic tensions in the world today, and given that religions find themselves caught up in these tensions, and even used at times to promote these tensions, there is need for interreligious dialogue on a global scale, and this need has never been more compelling. So, what Cardinal Arinze shares in this book about his experience of dialogue around the world is extremely timely and helpful for fostering greater interreligious understanding today, and for guiding religious persons in their common effort toward building peace and justice.

One strength of this book is that the interview format provides opportunities for Cardinal Arinze to discuss a number of different issues regarding interreligious dialogue in ways that are accessible to anyone who has an interest in the dialogue. Another strength is the fact that Cardinal Arinze speaks from his personal experience of addressing the challenges and the promises of interfaith encounter in our age of globalization and pluralism. His examples of dialogue in the context of inculturization in Africa and Asia are extremely helpful to those who wish to frame dialogue in ways that are most fruitful for all involved. He also gives the reader glimpses into the practical work of the Vatican's Pontifical Council for Interreligious Dialogue, as well as his own meetings with leaders of many religious traditions of the world.

Of special interest are Cardinal Arinze's views concerning the need for a "cultural dialogue" with Islam about shared values, the need for addressing religious extremism, intolerance, and fanaticism, the need for supporting religious freedom and human rights, the need to understand better the indigenous religious of Africa, and the need for better formation and more available information to enable clergy and laity alike to contribute to improved interreligious relations on the local, national and global levels of encounter. In these pages, the reader will also find both encouragement and guidance in the clear and frank ways Cardinal Arinze presents a theology of salvation that promotes the forms and goals of interreligious dialogue while avoiding the pitfalls of relativism and syncretism.

Cardinal Arinze has a gift for speaking to both the veteran practitioner of interreligious dialogue as well as the hesitant beginner. He is able to speak clearly and honestly about his own experience in dialogue while offering the advice of the Catholic Church on how such dialogue can be both authentic and fruitful. His words in this book give the reader confidence that authentic dialogue can deepen rather than water down one's own faith. His words also give hope that the fruits of authentic interreligious dialogue are contributing today to building a more united and peaceful world community.

Donald W. Mitchell
Purdue University

A Dialogue —
Not a Religious
Supermarket

Conversation in
the Global Village

Our world has become a "global village" in terms of politics, the economy, and especially information technology. Is this also true for relationships among religions?

That is certainly true of relationships among religions. People travel more today than ever before, some for business, pleasure or study, others because of political problems in their homelands. Traveling has become relatively simple. Today one can fly quickly to any place on earth. People bring their religion with them and meet others who profess the same or a different religion. More than ever, people of different religious persuasions have the chance to encounter one another, sometimes briefly, sometimes for extended periods of time. Even those who do not travel will run into people of a different religion at home. From a religious viewpoint the world has become pluralistic. That is the situation in which we are living today.

Political, social and economic relationships also have a religious dimension. Even many modern crises have a religious context. We therefore must ask ourselves how well human problems can be surmounted if we do not take this basic fact into account.

The fact is that we cannot fully comprehend human relationships without considering their religious context. It is necessary to recognize the religious dimension in human relationships in order to understand the human person and human behavior. Whether this religious context is immediately apparent or not does not really matter. We still must be aware of it and keep it in mind.

Understanding the fundamental religious aspect of human life helps us realize the complex causes of conflict. Many of these causes are apparent; others are not. Take for example the conflict in Indonesia, or the Kosovo situation, or other conflicts in the Balkan tinderbox, especially Bosnia-Herzegovina. Take Sudan, Somalia, Algeria, the conflict in the southern Philippines or the European conflict in northern Ireland. Or take my own country, Nigeria, especially in the north. Or take what seems to be the Kurds' ethnic conflict. The causes of these conflicts sometimes reach far back in history. Only a careful analysis of the factors that have led to these problems can bring us to a balanced judgment about them.

In all the conflicts I mentioned, religion plays a clear role. If you want to find a lasting solution for these challenges — I prefer to call them challenges rather than conflicts — and overlook or deny the religious dimension, you can hardly be called a realist. Human beings are quite thoroughly religious. Religion brings factors to bear in human behavior that differ from the motives the sciences or mathematics offer. People are ready to put their lives on the line for religious convictions, but never for mathematical issues. Religion motivates people to action; it gets them involved. An attack on religion is always an attack on the way people think of themselves and their society.

Religion is certainly not the only factor that determines human relations, but it certainly is a significant one. If we do not recognize the complex roots of today's conflicts in their multiple dimensions, we will not be able to come up with lasting solutions.

If what you say is true, doesn't every person have a duty to engage in religious dialogue?

Certainly. Our times call for interreligious dialogue that goes beyond academic discussion among representatives of various religions. We need a dialogue that extends deeply into all aspects of human relationships. That kind of interreligious dialogue must come first if we are to find ways to resolve religious conflicts.

I would go a step further. Dialogue is even necessary when there is no conflict. It is simply a question of how we think about human beings. To take people seriously means to take their religion seriously as well. It is not enough to engage in religious dialogue only when necessary for putting out the fires of conflict. No, we have to do better than that. We have to take the human person seriously in every aspect of being human. So interreligious dialogue is not just an insurance policy against conflict, it has value for its own sake.

How would you define interreligious dialogue? People seem to have very different ideas about what it really is.

Interreligious dialogue can be described in various ways. Usually, it begins when people of different religious convictions meet one another. The exchange that follows should not be only a meeting of "heads," but above all a meeting of "hearts." Dialogue proceeds when both sides are ready to accept each other. Acceptance means first of all listening to someone whose religious convictions differ from one's own. In itself, that is not easy.

Too many people today do not know how to listen. They only want to talk. They seem to have forgotten that God gave us two ears, but one mouth. Perhaps he wants us to listen twice as much as we speak. But today many people speak twice as much as they listen. First of all, then, interreligious dialogue means listening and trying to understand.

It also means approaching the other with a sympathetic attitude. This has nothing to do with pity or superiority. If one's partner in such a dialogue responds in the same way, communication takes place. There is cooperation. Respect and love for one another are possible.

Yes, real love. This is how it is: the more we love others, the more we understand them. When we do not love others, it is difficult to understand them. A mother understands her child better than anyone else because no one loves a child more than a mother.

Unfortunately, when many people hear of interreligious dialogue, they think only of intellectual discussion. They envision an international symposium of learned people who make lengthy, grandiose presentations with long bibliographies. Each professor proceeds in the same way and at the end all these words of wisdom are bound together into a thick volume. Naturally, such symposia constitute one kind of dialogue, but they are only a very small aspect of dialogue.

Most people who engage in interreligious dialogue are not scholars and professors; many cannot express their basic religious convictions in a coherent way. I assure you, if you ask average believers for a complete explanation of the essentials of their religion, or how their religion is expressed in worship and how it affects daily life, only a small percentage can give an answer that would hold up under examination by theologians. But that is not necessary in interreligious dialogue. That kind of thing comprises only a very small area of dialogue.

In referring to the main area of interreligious dialogue today, we use the term, "dialogue of life." This involves people of different religious convictions meeting each other in daily life. This can happen in the family; it happens more and more in the workplace, and has become common after work hours as well. Seldom do theological discussions take place, but people are communicating. Together, they engage in all kinds of common activities — for example in social or political life, in organizations, and in other kinds of service to their fellow human beings. This "dialogue of daily life," this "dialogue of love" is one form of interreligious dialogue.

The second is the dialogue of social interchange. People of different religions find themselves together in an attempt to successfully resolve some community venture. While common actions such as these do not involve theological discussion, they do engage the religious convictions of people on both sides; they involve the way they relate to the ideals of their religion. I can give you many examples from Africa, where people, inspired by their religion, come together precisely as believers to produce positive change in their living conditions. The "academic dialogue" we described earlier occurs seldom or never. Yet it is a form of real dialogue.

Another form is that of "spiritual dialogue." This happens, for example, when monks of different religions share their spiritual experiences with one another. This form of dialogue is also not about academic discussions, but rather about visiting each other, living together and learning from the spiritual experiences of each other. I could give many examples, but let me offer just one: numerous spiritual dialogues between our Trappist monks and Buddhist monks have borne fruit.

You see, these are all forms of interreligious dialogue. The name "interreligious relations," would perhaps describe them more accurately.

Can we call this "ecumenism"? Should this term be used to refer to activity done in common among various kinds of Christians, or can it be used to describe interreligious dialogue between Christians and non-Christians?

To stay with precise terminology, the term "ecumenism" refers specifically to relations among Christians. Using the term "ecumenism" to refer to dialogue among different religions would lead to confusion. Ecumenical activity is directed to ultimate Christian unity, according to the will of Christ. That kind of unity is not, nor can it be the goal of interreligious dialogue.

I would like to return to our discussion of interreligious dialogue. Some people have fundamentally different concepts of God. Are there limits to who can be discussion partners, or can interreligious dialogue include people of any faith?

You touch on an important point. Every interreligious discussion presumes that you know the essential beliefs of your partner. Only then will the boundaries for this dialogue become clear.

In Jewish-Christian dialogue it will likely become clear quite quickly how much both religions have in common; in Christian-Muslim dialogue there are also common elements, even though not as many as with Jews.

In the dialogue between Christians and those who belong to the traditional nature religions, the shared elements are still fewer. The same is true for Hinduism, which has a clear concept of God but not a clear-cut understanding of God as person. This context is different also when we get to Christian-Buddhist dialogue.

Partners in interreligious dialogue need to be aware of these differences, especially when they share significant similarities in faith and the concept of God. This is also true in comparing rites and forms of worship. Those who attempt dialogue without recognizing each other's differences enter such a discussion with invalid premises that can hardly lead to fruitful results.

What is the real object of this discourse among theologians of different religions? For example, Catholics consider the doctrine of the Trinity the heart of their faith but Muslims cannot accept such a dogma, or may even consider it scandalous. How far can such a discussion get? Are there limits to what the dialogue can address?

Basically, it is not advisable to begin a dialogue — on any of these levels — by first addressing such differences in faith. Psychologically that is a poor route to take. Even when all sides are theologically competent and well prepared, the discussion should always begin with areas of agreement, not with differences.

Let's stay with the things you mentioned. When Christians and Muslims discuss theological questions, I think they should begin with the concept of God. There is only one God, who has created us and to whom we owe obedience. At the end of our lives we will have to answer to him at the judgment. On these things, Christians and Muslims basically agree. So this is where we begin. On some questions, there is partial agreement: God sent his prophets to us. But here too we soon come to differences over the rank or importance of individual prophets. So it would not be advisable to go deeply into this at the beginning. But these are basic areas where a dialogue can open. From here we begin to see how many common elements Christians and Muslims actually share in the basic faith deposit.

Nevertheless, there are areas of faith where we find huge differences. For Christians and Muslims this may include belief in the Holy Trinity or in Jesus as Son of God, as true man and true God, or in the death of God's son on the cross. Muslims cannot accept that, and so it would not be wise to open an interreligious dialogue with such controversial issues. Or take, for example, the role of Mary, the mother of God. The Koran mentions Mary thirty-four times, always with respect and love, as the virgin mother of Jesus, but never as the "Mother of God." So why should a discussion with Muslims begin with such deep and difficult mysteries of faith? I am convinced, however, that it is possible for a group of theologians who know and respect each other well enough and have established a climate of mutual trust even to address questions like that.

Faith Is Not Negotiable

*A*re any topics really taboo?

Even under the conditions I just mentioned, any topic can come up in a dialogue, but that does not mean that we Catholics can in any way "negotiate" the central mysteries of our faith. Besides that, many central mysteries of our faith are so deep that they remain quite beyond our grasp and cannot be subjects for debate. A discussion on the mystery of the Holy Trinity in the light of pure reason alone with someone who does not believe in it would be very difficult and unadvisable? Dialogue with those who belong to non-Christian religions does not mean "negotiating" with them. Faith mysteries are necessarily clothed in inadequate human words, concepts and images — and can be presented only at the end of patient, trustful and fruitful dialogues.

The ecumenical dialogue between the Roman Catholic Church and the other Christian Churches — Orthodox, Anglican, Lutheran and other Reform Churches — has advanced greatly since the Second Vatican Council. The dialogue among the mono-

theistic religions — Christian, Muslim, Jewish — has at least found a strong, institutional framework and has already produced considerable results. What is the situation with those who do not have a personal belief in God, who view God not as a person but perhaps as a higher power, as in most religions of Asia?

Obviously it is harder to reach understanding between Christians and adherents of religions who do not have a personal God. That is likewise true of these religions' contacts with Jews and Muslims. The understanding between Christians and adherents of religions who share with them faith in a personal God is certainly easier. Yet patient and enduring love can find ways that lead us to common goals as, for example, through social concerns and questions such as family issues and child rearing. In these areas all religions share a common commitment. Understandably, topics of dogma are much more difficult. But I would like to reiterate that where trust has grown and where people are competent and well-prepared, even difficult questions can be discussed.

When partners have fundamental differences on basic faith issues, isn't the dialogue limited more or less to presenting one's own position?

That is true. Where such fundamental differences exist, the boundaries for dialogue quickly become apparent. Then we must be content with reaching agreement on practical issues, which in itself is something significant.

What are the pre-conditions for carrying on meaningful dialogue?

Oh, they are many. I would list, for example, freedom of faith and worship. Significant religious dialogue can develop only when the participants feel neither fear nor pressure. Real dialogue is difficult in places burdened with tension among various religions.

Dialogue is not absolutely impossible in these cases, but it certainly is more difficult.

Another important requirement for meaningful interreligious dialogue is that the partners be authentic and faithful representatives of their own religion. Those who lack sufficient knowledge of their own religion cannot carry on a dialogue with other religions. Imagine diplomats who do not know the policy of their own country but attempt to represent it abroad. Individuals who disagree with some of the tenets of their own religion could not participate successfully in interreligious dialogue. A clear identity is a very important condition for meaningful dialogue.

Naturally, solid knowledge is important too. Those who have good will but an inadequate concept of their own religion run a high risk as they try to negotiate the slippery slopes of discussion with adherents of other religions. A foundation of sound knowledge is indispensable. Also, one's intentions must be honorable. Intrigue, intellectual trickery, or hypocrisy do not make for good partners in dialogue. Dialogue requires openness, reliability and integrity. Partners in interreligious dialogue must have the confidence that they know clearly where each other stands. Then they can move from that surety to the realization that mutual trust is possible. These are some of the conditions that must precede meaningful dialogue.

What particular contribution can Christians bring to interreligious dialogue?

Christians can make a huge contribution to interreligious dialogue — they possess a rich heritage of faith. They bring the example of Jesus Christ, who came into the world not to establish a local village religion but to proclaim a new family, the family composed of all the children of God. This religion has been received by people and societies all over the world and has been integrated into every culture. We represent a universal faith rooted in the fatherhood of God and that embodied in the human form by Jesus Christ. Christians can bring all of that into interreligious dialogue. They can also bring countless rich theological formulations about God and humanity — from the days of Saint Paul until now. Think also of the teachings that our Church has articulated over the past two millennia — not just on internal matters, but on community and social issues, on scientific problems, on human rights, on the whole area of justice and peace in society. Christians can and should contribute all of these riches to interreligious dialogue.

You have described the Christian contribution to dialogue, but the word "dialogue" itself implies that it is not a one-way street. What can Christians expect from their partners in interreligious dialogue?

Of course, dialogue is not a one-way street. We give and we receive. Every religion in the world has left its imprint on its cultural environment. How can one begin to explore the culture of Thailand without understanding something about Buddhism? How can one understand the Arab world without knowing about Islam? How can one understand Japanese culture without studying Shintoism and Buddhism? How can one understand the culture of India without exploring Hinduism? Cultures are suffused with the religious. Christians can come to respect and understand other cultures only if they know the respective religious contexts.

I will give you an example. Many religions in Asia take the human body much more seriously than we do in the West. Japanese and Chinese are aware of the influence that bodily postures, such as a certain way of sitting, can have on the mental state. Christians must take such findings seriously.

Also, the great variety of forms of worship can offer inspiration. I am thinking, for example, of forms of meditation, of forms of reverence such as bowing or offering incense, of meditation aids like prayer cords that seem to date back earlier than our rosary — these are simply ways of helping one concentrate on God. In the area of inculturation Christians can take inspiration from non-Christian religions. However, basic philosophical convictions such as reincarnation pose fundamental obstacles.

Through your service to the Church you have been able to gain insights through your contacts with other religions. Could you describe the work of the Pontifical Council for Interreligious Dialogue? Practically speaking, how would you describe your job? What do you do on a day-to-day basis?

Practically speaking, we work in three areas. First, we see what can be done to make other religions and beliefs better known among Christians. This entails the opposite as well, as we look for opportunities to improve the way we communicate knowledge of Christianity to other religions. That can happen in many ways, for example, by ongoing meetings here in Rome with representatives of other religions, or by visiting non-Christian faith communities. This also includes encouraging the study of non-Christian religions. Our small office staff cannot possibly know everything. We encourage the education and study of experts, not just in Rome, but all over the world. Such education goes beyond what the normal seminary program for priests can include. It requires experts from various university faculties. Part of this first area includes encouraging international symposia among scholars in the various disciplines. We also encourage the publication of books relating interreligious dialogue. In a nutshell, our first task might be called improving the flow of information about each other on both sides.

Secondly, we work within the universal Church at all its levels — from the national bishops' conferences, to the individual dioceses, even to the smallest parish units. Our discussion partners also include Catholic faculties, seminaries and religious orders. We want to engage all these people, groups and organizations in dialogue and encourage them to meet with the believers of other religions.

Our staff numbers only twelve. By ourselves, we are too few to conduct dialogue with the adherents of all the world's religions. Even if we could, it would not be in line with the policy of the Holy Father, who leaves intact the primary responsibility for directing the different ways of enriching Church life to the local churches, to the bishops' conferences, and to the individual bishops. The Holy Father wants us to encourage all offices of the Church to engage in dialogue. This task is not just ours but everyone's. I would place this second aspect of our work under the general heading, "animating, encouraging and raising consciousness."

In practice, that happens in a variety of ways. For example, when the bishops come to Rome every five years for their *ad limina* visit, we try to speak especially with those who have a variety of different religions in their territory. It often happens that those bishops or bishops' conferences invite our staff to help them come up with ways to encourage or conduct interreligious dialogue in their areas. We also maintain regular contact with Catholic universities and encourage them to promote interreligious dialogue.

Seminaries all over the world play an especially important role in this. The clergy of the future need two things: formation and information, especially about non-Catholic religions. Most important is their ability to approach people of other religious convictions and to be able to conduct expert, tactful discussion with them. Generally we encourage dialogue, but sometimes we must intervene or correct dialogue that has entered into questionable territory.

I would call our third area intracurial. When matters touching on other religions arise in one of our offices here in Rome, we try to offer advice and direct help. This work continues far beyond what is reported in newspapers. Ultimately, all of us at the Vatican share responsibility to serve Christ and the Church, although in different ways. I see no danger of unemployment.

Can you describe your experience with representatives of other religions? How do such discussions go? Is there a polite distance, or is it friendly and cordial? How do you get along with your partners in dialogue?

It varies. There can be short polite visits, like those I make to Muslim dignitaries when I am in an African country where Islam plays a large role. Such polite visits seldom lead to any profound exchange. They are really gestures of goodwill.

However, it is quite different at our annual discussions with the representatives of the four great international Islamic organizations: the World Muslim League, the World Muslim Congress, the International Organization for Dawa and Relief and the Organization of the Islamic Conference. We meet with these organizations regularly, one year at a place of our choice, another of theirs. We keep to a pre-established schedule, with experts from both sides sharing the podium, and presenting well-prepared talks. We allow plenty of time for dialogue, and we discuss even political issues and problems quite openly. Our goal is to create a genuine basis of trust that can then lead to our working together to serve others.

These meetings are essentially different from the short, polite visits I described. We try to discuss controversial topics calmly, but that always depends on the participants. The longstanding problems in a particular locality, we realize, can only be addressed and resolved by the local people delving deeply into the heart of the issue.

In a "Dialogue of Common Action" religion could be considered irrelevant. For example, when an emergency or catastrophe arises, simple human compassion may lead people to work together on behalf of those who are suffering. Even humanitarians with no religion are capable of such actions. What difference do you see between motivation that is merely humanitarian and that of a religious person?

From the viewpoint of the believer the question is easy to answer. Our motivation comes from our religion. As Christians we could say that we follow the example of Jesus Christ and the commandment to love our neighbor. We try to meet Jesus in each person. That is certainly more than humanitarianism; it is part of my religion. If I take others seriously and respect them as I help them, then I am giving witness to Christ. Mission has many faces. It does not mean just proclaiming the gospel, but also service to all people, helping those in need, intervening for the sake of justice and peace as well as engaging in interreligious dialogue. Consider Mother Teresa. She and her sisters never preached; they simply showed love for the poor, the hungry and dying. That shows an authentic witness for Jesus Christ. Mother Teresa made this memorable statement: "All those people who lie here at the side of the street are Jesus, waiting for our love." Care for these poorest of the poor is certainly a religious act, even if it is not preaching in the traditional sense. This total love of neighbor is an integral part of our religion, not something added on.

Is such "dialogue of common action" — for the Catholic Church — a relatively new form of relating to other world religions?

That this has become so much a part of our conscious intention is certainly new. But it is not new in the real sense of the word. Take Saint Francis, for example. As he sent his brothers out into that part of the world that today we call the Near East, he told them expressly to be friendly toward the Muslims. Francis opposed any hostility toward Muslims. He opposed the crusades. We could consider him a patron of interreligious dialogue, since that was his purpose — as a way of giving witness to Christ, naturally.

*I*s *he an exception?*

In the degree of his sensitivity to others, he certainly was an exception. Most missionaries in centuries after Francis's time went out to preach Christ. In those days they generally refrained from the sort of interreligious dialogue that has become commonplace in *our* times. But to be fair to them, we need to realize that intensive study of other religions is a rather recent practice.

You see, for centuries the center of Christianity was Europe, even though Jesus Christ was born in the Near East and had to flee from Herod's persecution to Africa. Nevertheless, after Paul preached the gospel in Europe, Christian philosophy and classical theology flourished there, all the way down to our own times. Europe was self-contained and content with itself.

On the other hand, centuries ago there was nothing like the mobility of today. Travel was difficult, and far-reaching communication was practically non-existent. What did anyone really know about the religions of Asia? Even less was known about the traditional religions of Africa. The world was very Eurocentric. After Columbus' "discovery" this European perspective led to calling America the "New World." What was known of Africa? Only North Africa, and that only as far as the great barrier of the Sahara. No one knew of anything to the south.

European history books state that Nigeria was "discovered" in 1795. I would add, "Oh yes, I discovered England in 1955." You see, each of us has a very subjective view of the world.

Ignorance, combined with a European outlook, resulted in very little being known about the religions of other continents. Today that has changed fundamentally. Now we have an entirely different basis for meaningful dialogue among religions than there was in past centuries, and that is not meant as a reproach.

One more thing. Today people and cultures are mingling to a degree never experienced before. That provides a new challenge for the theological dialogue with other religions. Today, a theology that ignores the religious plurality of the world is unthinkable. A charismatic figure like John XXIII clearly realized that, and that is why he gave so much attention to this issue at the Council. He charged the Church to find out what people of different religions held in common. Paul VI, in his encyclical *Ecclesiam suam,* used the beautiful image of concentric circles. Christ is at the center, and at various distances around this center stand the Christian confessions, the monotheistic religions and then the other religious convictions. Later papal writings develop this image further, most dynamically in the Council's constitution, *Lumen gentium,* which explains that the saving work of Christ operates in view of all humanity, not just for Christians.

I would like to address another form of dialogue, one I would call the "dialogue of religious experience." This form began on a simple level and still continues. I am thinking of the shared experience of contemplative life, such as that which the late British Benedictine Bede Griffith undertook and experienced in the Hindu region of India, or that which Trappists and Buddhist monks have shared more recently.

This is indeed a significant part of dialogue. Nevertheless, it is a form of dialogue that requires careful preparation on the part of the participants. Father Bede Griffith had to be a better than average Benedictine; he had to be able to live his Benedictine spirituality, the theology of his order; he had to know the history of its piety so as to avoid the considerable risks of such an experiment. One who is well prepared can have a worthwhile experience in such a dialogue. While it is good to be enthusiastic about an idea, this is not enough. What is important is careful intellectual, spiritual and theological preparation. The intensity and duration of such an experiment is also significant. It is quite different to spend one day in a Buddhist monastery, than to spend several weeks or months in an ashram in India, or engage in a long-term sharing of contemplation with monks of different religions.

Christians and non-Christians have lived next to each other without acknowledging one another for almost two thousand years. When they did come into contact, it has not always been with respect and love. Sometimes it has erupted into violence and religious war.

Unfortunately that is true, but it is consistent — even outside the area of religion — with the general mind-set of earlier societies. The idea of free communication and nonviolent resolution of conflict has emerged relatively recently in history. Even today it does not prevail universally. Religious violence is directed not only toward those of a different religion. In the Middle Ages, even within the same religion, those who did not keep the rules as dictated by the authorities were identified as a danger to the social order and persecuted.

While I do not advocate a religious shopping mall where everything on display is of comparable value, I am convinced that increased respect for the religion of others is something positive. I can respect the content of other faith convictions, even though I cannot follow them personally.

The Church need not lose anything at all through this new attitude toward non-Christian religions. On the contrary, I believe she has gained very much.

Religion Is Not
Just a Private Matter

Some people strive to be friendly with people of other faiths, but maintain that religion is strictly a personal matter, something to be practiced privately. They respect and tolerate other religions, but don't seek to discover their material content. Some would maintain that one religion is as good as another. Doesn't such an opinion subvert the real purpose of interreligious dialogue that follows the different levels that we have been discussing?

Certainly religion has a private dimension; it cannot, however, be separated from its public aspects. God did not create people as individuals without relationships, circumscribed within themselves. God has created us as social beings. That is part of our nature. God's saving work is not directed to us just as individuals, but as part of humanity. We do not define ourselves just as individual beings but as family, as a people, as church. Along with the individual dimension, religion always has a public and social dimension. That is why I am mistaken if I make religion into a private matter, as though faith were something

43

contraband, to be dealt with as secretly as possible. A religion that I hide is, in my opinion, not authentic. Religion requires profession. It is not in keeping with human nature to reduce religion to an exclusively private matter.

The Second Vatican Council has given interreligious dialogue a new and important dimension. We could say, therefore, that interreligious dialogue follows from the explicit desire and wishes of the Church. Do other religions share similar views?

Some do share such views, but others do not. In all honesty, for a long time many religions have not held the same view of dialogue as the Catholic Church. The Catholic Church has developed a clearly formulated theology, that provides motivation for dialogue with adherents of other religions. But some religions have no clear concept of associating with those who hold other religious convictions. Some religions may seem to welcome dialogue but in reality use it to indoctrinate others who do not share their faith. We are quite aware of such differences as we seek dialogue with other religions.

Does the Catholic Church encourage interreligious dialogue with the idea that meeting people of other faiths can be enriching for Christians?

This question needs more than a brief answer. We do not seek dialogue because we have doubts about our own faith, or because we find some deficiency in it. Rather, with Saint Paul we say, "We know whom we believe in: Jesus Christ." We seek dialogue with adherents of other religions because we are motivated first of all by love for others, and because of the esteem that flows from this love. So in that sense we can say that it is part of our faith.

Meeting with other religions can lead us to reexamine our faith and to reflect anew on our own religion. The strong and deep faith of many adherents of other religions may shame us in the light of our own weaknesses of faith, and challenge us to resolve them.

I would say that dialogue should lead not to a kind of new teaching, but to mutual enrichment. The way in which others speak of their faith, pass it on, and celebrate worship, can inspire and enrich me. Above all, many useful suggestions and incentives for the Church's work of inculturation can grow out of dialogue. The pope said this too, calling other religions "a positive challenge for the Church" (*Redemptoris missio,* 56).

Other religions invite us to take a second look at our identity. Interreligious dialogue leads the Church to rediscover the fullness of the gifts that the Spirit of God has entrusted to her. In addition, dialogue helps us realize in a positive way how the Holy Spirit can also be active in other cultures, religions and peoples.

How far can Catholics go in embracing theological formulations, forms of spiritual life, and liturgy that we discover through our encounters with other religions? In the past wouldn't we have been counseled against accepting concepts from other religions because to do so would constitute "syncretism?"

That is very difficult to answer in the abstract. We would have to know exactly what is involved before we could say, "This is a case of syncretism."

I would prefer to put it this way: One thing is the Christian faith, and that needs to stand firm. Another thing is the way in which this faith is expressed; in this there is room for variation.

The Christian faith certainly will find a different expression in Asia than it does in Africa or Europe. In its essence it is the same everywhere, but the manner of articulation, of living and celebrating it can be different. To be sure, it must remain identifiable as the same faith. While it is entirely legitimate to recognize people as American Catholics, Nigerian Catholics, and Indian Catholics, they must remain identifiable as Catholics. I know, however, that this is easier said than done. But I think it is possible.

Certainly, every attempt at inculturation poses some danger of syncretism. The local churches have a great responsibility here, as do theologians, bishops, and naturally the Church authorities here in Rome. As with many good things, inculturation has two sides; it involves risk as well as opportunity.

That, by the way, applies not just to the faith; it is also true in daily life. To drive a car or take a plane is in itself a good thing. At the same time, no one can deny that such activities involve a certain measure of risk. So there is our answer: avoid dangers when possible, drive safely, and don't fly head-on into a storm.

But to return to your question. I consider inculturation to be an extremely important task for the Church of the future, but we must go carefully so as not to end up in relativism, or some kind of religious hodgepodge or a lukewarm blend of all religions. Certainly, I hope that through inculturation the authentic faith will be translated appropriately into each culture. . . .

Interreligious dialogue is always going to be more difficult where religion is established as a "state religion," where being an Arab, for example, means being a Muslim, or being Indian means being a Hindu. We can be self-critical here, since for a long time in Catholic missionary work — and the churches of the reformation were no different — being Christian meant accepting European culture or at least European forms of civilization.

You have touched a sore point; what you say is true. When we encounter religions that are identified with the ethnicity of their faithful, inculturation is practically impossible for the Church. An Indian saying that one must be a Hindu to be a "good" Indian or a Thai starting out with the idea that one can be a good Thai only by being a Buddhist, presents a position that we cannot accept. These natural biases do exist. There are those who say that an Arab can only be Muslim. There are also such biases in Africa, where many nationalists say that being an authentic African requires the profession of traditional African religion. We cannot and will not in any way accept that. But you are right; such mistakes have been made and, unfortunately, will.

. . . even on the part of Christians.

Yes, unfortunately that has happened historically, but not very often in the case of Christians.

Even down to our own time such cultural biases have found expression in many forms that at best can be amusing, at worst upsetting. For example, at one time acceptance of the Christian faith included outward imitation of Europeans, even to the kind of garment worn at baptism.

Yes, the Church has made such mistakes in some places. However, the Church also has a long tradition of tolerance. In 1659, when the then "Propagation of the

Faith," today's Congregation for the Evangelization of Peoples, sent missionaries to Indochina, it gave these messengers of the faith explicit instructions to esteem and respect all that they found good in the local culture. Apparently they were further advanced than later generations, for they were already urging missionaries to respect the local culture and to oppose only that which could not be reconciled with the Christian faith. These missionaries were not emissaries of Spanish, French or Italian culture but messengers of Christ. Just imagine — that was as early as 1659. Think of people like Giovanni di Montecorvino, Matteo Ricci or Roberto de Nobili, truly great men. Today, we can see that they were pioneers of inculturation. However, in those days they were greatly misunderstood and thwarted, even by members of their own religious communities. But at least, alongside the negative examples, we do find such positive models.

I would like to relate an example from my own homeland. When we were baptized as youngsters, we took baptismal names. Quite naturally most of us chose English names. Somewhere in our heads was nestled the idea that to be a Christian automatically meant to accept a European name. Today we think quite differently and have a much better understanding. Today we give children African names, which can indeed also be Christian. My family name "Arinze," which my father received from his father, actually stands for *Arinze Chukwu,* and that means "Thanks be to God," "*Deo gratias.*" That is certainly a wonderful Christian name. Why must one take an English or some other European name? It is a positive thing, however, to choose for baptism the name of a saint as our heavenly patron and model. The saints are our brothers and sisters in the faith.

But it has taken a relatively long time for us to see it that way. So today many theologians in the newer churches are promoting a "Theology of Inculturation," a very recent development.

We can understand how missionaries in past times made mistakes when they did not have today's insights. Every science advances, including the science of theology. We have developed much better ways and means of expressing and explaining the faith, and making it intelligible in different cultures. However it is much easier to enunciate the principles of inculturation than to translate them into practice.

Can we say in principle that the Christian faith can be lived authentically in all cultures?

I can answer that question with an unqualified yes. If we could not say that, we would have to doubt that God sent the Son as savior for all people of every time and culture.

In 1986, you already established that point in an address to the German Catholic Mission Council in Würzburg. At that time, you said evangelization respects the culture of every people. Despite your clear statement, though, I do have some doubts. Isn't that too broad of a generalization? Many cultures, such as in Africa and elsewhere, include polygamy. This is hardly approved by the Church, nor are many initiation and burial rites. In his book, Our Strange Gods, *your fellow Nigerian bishop, Godfrey Okoye of Port Harcourt, judged such practices harshly.*

My statement that the Church respects the culture of every people is valid and correct, but I would add the qualification that such respect must be paid only to the good elements of a culture. The gospel would contradict itself in accepting indiscriminately every element of every culture and giving it a blessing. Every culture of the world contains some elements that cannot be reconciled with the gospel of Jesus Christ. That is why it is so important to study a culture well and know it thoroughly in all its aspects, positive and negative. Then one can examine all the elements of a culture in the light of the gospel.

When elements in a culture are incompatible with the gospel, we cannot change the gospel; the elements of the culture must change. That applies to polygamy, for example, which is found in many places in Africa. Polygamy is incompatible with the gospel and therefore unacceptable.

In some African cultures twins were denied the right to live. These cultures considered twins unnatural and killed them. In fact the mother was punished as well. This kind of thing is unacceptable. Any doctor today can give the medical explanation for how twins are formed in the womb. It certainly is not unnatural. So the way some cultures treat twins will never be accepted by the Church, any more than it would find human sacrifice acceptable, which also was a practice in certain cultures. For example, when a great chieftain died, the people were convinced that he could not go alone into the land of the spirits; he needed companions. So people were offered in sacrifice, usually his wife or wives or his servant. That sort of thing is completely incompatible with the Christian faith.

In this regard, I do not even need to refer to specific Christian doctrines; it is a simple question of human dignity. Human sacrifice directly contradicts human dignity. The same is true of polygamy. It is opposed to the human dignity of the woman. In objecting to polygamy I do not need to allude specifically to any Christian concepts.

It would also be a mistake to look only to Africa for such elements incompatible with Christianity. Europe has them too. To my mind, for example, the strong trend in European culture toward complete secularization has little compatibility with Christianity. Or when children in Europe take second place to material possessions, or when house pets often receive more affection than children, these elements of European culture or Western civilization are incompatible with Christianity. Here again, it is less a question of Christian faith than simple human dignity. It is absurd to be hauled into court for killing a cat, when it is considered acceptable to kill a child in the womb.

I would also add that putting homosexual couples on an equal status with families, or the practice of euthanasia, are entirely unacceptable elements in any civilization or culture.

To summarize my position, then, on one hand the gospel must respect cultures, but on the other it must put them to the test and weigh them.

But, Cardinal Arinze, would you say straight out to an African who lives in polygamy with several wives and who truly cares for them, "My friend, you are living in mortal sin"?

The situation that you describe is objectively sinful, but subjectively it might be seen quite differently. You see, most polygamists in Africa were not yet Christians at the time they entered polygamous marriages. Their tradition allowed them to live with several wives. So they have taken two, three or four in completely good conscience. If that is so, I think one can leave judgment of this arrangement safely in God's hands.

When a polygamist becomes Christian, he and his community must look for steps toward a solution. As a Christian he can only live with one wife, but that does not relieve him of responsibility for the others. He must continue to provide for them, if they still need his financial help, even though they no longer have a sexual relationship. Obviously his responsibility extends to the children of these unions. When he accepts this solution, then he and all the wives from his polygamous marriage may be admitted to the sacraments. In any case this is what I always did as archbishop of Onitsha. But it is impossible for him to live in a sexual relationship with all his wives and still go to the sacraments. That won't do. Such questions must be resolved responsibly and always with gentleness and respect for human dignity.

Other issues are involved with the marriage contract. Some African theologians and missionaries would like the Church to approve African-style marriages, which are done in stages. Can you accept such practices?

That depends on what you mean by marriage in stages. It is not acceptable for two unmarried young people to live together as though they were already husband and wife. But if by marriage in stages you mean the traditional rites that precede the Christian marriage contract — for example, negotiating a marriage contract or transfer of the bride's dowry — then that is something entirely different. It is up to the local church to examine these rites and determine whether they are acceptable or not.

The ministers of the sacrament of marriage, as is well known, are the bridal couple themselves. When they conclude the contract and the Church has witnessed this, the marriage is valid and they can live together as husband and wife. The form that they use can change, but the reality itself does not. The traditional canonical marriage contract could be augmented with traditional. The African Synod of 1994 said that the local churches have full authority in this area.

Some in Africa have the idea that a marriage is not complete until the wife has borne children. Having children is very important for the African family. So a young man and his wife live together on trial, as it were, until she becomes pregnant. Then they are ready for a formal concluding of the contract. I do not think this practice and the ideas behind it are in keeping with the human dignity of the woman. It turns a woman into an object. I think that young people who wish to marry should trust that God will send them children. It may be a heavy burden for them if they are not able to have children, but a childless marriage can have its own blessings. Reducing women to breeding machines is not humane.

In this context I would like to raise another topic being discussed in the younger churches: celibacy.

The agenda for the bishops' synod of 1971 included celibacy. Cardinal Zoungrana, bishop of Ouagadougou, the capital of Burkina Faso, strongly objected at that time to the admission of married men to the priesthood or even to the diaconate, and he emphatically defended the obligation of celibacy for the Latin

Church. These observations of Cardinal Zoungrana were in strong contrast to those of the then archbishop of Kinshasa, Cardinal Malula, who spoke of the African mentality and wondered whether the idea of celibacy was compatible with it.

At that time, you supported the position of Cardinal Zoungrana and called celibacy "one of the most beautiful charisms of the Catholic Church." This position, which we all know is shared by the pope, is no longer viewed so uniformly in Europe and in North and Latin America — even inside the Church and among bishops — especially with regard to the diaconate. Do you still believe that the priesthood will remain celibate in the future, or do you think pastoral considerations could dictate alternatives?

My position on the question of celibacy has not changed since my participation in the bishops' synod of 1971 that you mentioned. Naturally we all know that celibacy is not of divine law but is a requirement determined by the Church, which values it for good reasons.

That it is not of divine law is evident from the fact that there are several rites in our Catholic Church that have no obligation of priestly celibacy. Because it is of ecclesiastical law rather than divine law it is entirely legitimate for two Catholic bishops to have different opinions about it.

But you asked about my opinion. I am convinced that there are better reasons for keeping celibacy than for giving it up. You see, for me the issue is whether someone in priestly service is ready for total commitment. The celibate priest is more devoted to Christ, the bridegroom of the Church.

I think we see a general tendency today to question the Church's norms. That is true not only of celibacy but also of divorce, abortion and other dictates of divine not ecclesiastical law. A Protestant bishop in the United States once told me, "Don't think that putting an end to celibacy will solve your problems. We do not have celibacy in our church and we still have problems with preaching and with the public conduct of clergy." If a priest is not ready to dedicate himself freely and totally to his vocation, then I am afraid that he will not be ready to do so if he were married.

Then, too, celibates often have an unrealistic notion of married life, as though marriage means only wedded bliss. There are trials and sufferings that come with living within a close human relationship. Not only celibacy requires sacrifice; married life can demand many sacrifices too. These are just a few considerations in support of celibacy; it would take a series of interviews to cover them all.

I would like to add a personal note. You see, I come from a culture that practices polygamy. Surprisingly, polygamy has given me a greater appreciation for the celibate lifestyle. You must understand that it is something extraordinary when someone consciously refrains from marriage in order to remain completely free for service. Celibacy as a total commitment to Christ is something that people who practice polygamy understand. For them a celibate priest who really lives this commitment has great credibility.

Nor should we recommend doing away with celibacy by pointing to broken vows. Regrettably that does happen. But we should not throw out the baby with the bath water. Look, we have many automobile accidents every day. It would be foolish to conclude that automobiles should therefore be outlawed. A sensible conclusion would be that people must learn to drive better. That is analogous to the celibate life. We can and must practice asceticism and learn to set aside our own personal interests and wishes in offering ourselves for others. If we do not do that, we can suffer celibate shipwreck.

You asked about deacons. That is an entirely different matter, because celibacy is not an issue. The Church has approved a married diaconate.

Africa has more priestly vocations than Europe, but still has a great shortage. How do things look for the future? What do you think of lay parish administrators?

. . . Parish administration involves many, many functions that are not bound up with the priesthood. Naturally, lay people could take on those responsibilities. . . . I would look positively on such a possibility as a temporary answer to our pastoral needs. But even if we approve such temporary solutions, we should not lose sight of the fact that we need priests. We must not stop praying for vocations, that in the future divine providence may provide the priests we need for our parishes. But before trying all kinds of substitute solutions, I must ask myself sincerely: have I done all I can to encourage priestly vocations when instructing children, visiting with our families, and also through my own prayer? As priests we must continue to ask ourselves: have we lived our priesthood so convincingly and appealingly that young men are inspired to see themselves called to the priestly life and pursue that vocation?

Have parents prayed that one of their children would become a priest, sister or brother? Have the children been living in a home where priests are treated with respect? Those are questions that we all must ask ourselves. It is not enough to complain about the priest shortage.

Also, we must look at the entire world picture. It is true that several parts of the world have a great priest shortage, but in other parts of the world the number of vocations is large. That means, I think, that we must develop a spirit of sharing.

You certainly have a shortage of priests, yet you send Nigerian priests to other parts of the world . . .

We are trying to create a spirit of sharing. There was a time when we had hardly any priests. We were receiving missionaries from Europe. Today we have more priests, so we share them generously with other churches. I will not say that we have enough priests in Nigeria, but we must learn to give, even before we are self-sufficient. The same is true for Kerala in India, which has a great number of priestly vocations. But none of us can see into the future; in a few years or decades the picture could be entirely different.

I would like to return to our discussion of the relationship between religion and culture. Frequently, the cathedral of Yamoussoukro, the "Concrete Saint Peter's" on the Ivory Coast has been criticized as an example of the lack of appreciation for native African culture and crass imitation of traditional European forms. Nevertheless, you have called it a "great church." Does this building show the right direction for church architecture in Africa?[1]

I would not use the Basilica in Yamoussoukro as an example of inculturation. It is not inculturation but imitation of a classic style. Yes, the church does attempt to

---

1. *Editor's Note:* Cardinal Arinze and his interviewer are discussing a political figure, Felix Houphoët-Boigny, past-president of the Ivory Coast. The cathedral at Yamoussoukro is the largest Christian church in the world, larger even than Saint Peter's in Rome.

imitate Saint Peter's in Rome. I wish it had turned out smaller. The daughter should not try to overshadow the mother. That is my first point.

But recall what I said at the opening of the Basilica. At that time, I said, "Holy Father, we Africans have a lot of poor people. We have people who do not have even a nice little cottage to call their own. Many do not have a house worthy of being called a home. Yet even the poor among us rejoice to see a beautiful church where they can worship erected in God's honor. Africans are not envious of the beauty of God's house. None of us would say a church is too expensive for God. That is how Africans rejoice over a grand and splendid church." When I spoke of a "great church," that is what I meant, and nothing else. Naturally I am against African imitations of churches like Saint Peter's or Saint Paul Outside the Walls, or the cathedral of Chartres or the cathedral of Cologne. That is not the way to go.

But people ask why so much money was spent in Yamoussoukro.

I would like to mention two things in this regard. First of all, had my opinion been sought beforehand, I would have suggested to use the money to build not one giant basilica but rather small parish churches for two hundred villages. Secondly, remember that the one who financed this church claimed that he was investing his own personal fortune there.

Had he extorted the money from his own people? As far as I know, no. Did he steal the money? Again, not as far as I know. Naturally, I am not the CIA. So accept the official explanation: a president of state was investing his own money there. As an aside, I would have to say that I prefer what he has done over the practice of many African chiefs of state who stash their money in Switzerland. This president chose to use his personal assets to build a church in his own country. Assuming that it was his own money, such a choice should not be called a problem.

Let me also add that when I visited the Basilica in 1996 I found, to my surprise, that it has become a pilgrimage center. The number of people who come to pray is beyond all expectations. People obviously feel drawn by the atmosphere of this place and come as pilgrims to pray. Symbols are very important. I know it was said at the time, "People on the Ivory Coast need bread, not churches." I answered, "My dear friend, those two things are not contradictory." What do we preach in the Basilica? Well, the spirit of sharing with the poor, so that those who have no bread may experience solidarity with their fellow Christians and receive bread. When someone buys bread for a certain amount of money and distributes it, hunger returns as soon as people have eaten. When we preach in order to change consciousness, we declare permanent war on hunger and privation.

Naturally the complaints about Yamoussoukro could be made about every basilica and cathedral in the world. The poor exist in every time and place in history, yet the magnificent cathedrals that people have built have become a cultural heritage for the entire world.

That would be my response to critics of the Basilica of Yamoussoukro. No one who has visited the cathedral can deny that it is impressive and has great esthetic appeal. Nonetheless, I repeat, my preference is for churches that emerge from the culture of the faithful.

The World Religions in the Divine Plan of Salvation

Let's return to the topic of dialogue. A great problem for the Catholic Church in Africa is the spread of countless "independent" churches and church-like communities. Their doctrine is partly Christian and partly a blend of traditional African elements. Has the Catholic Church established any official dialogue with such communities?

Such dialogue is extremely difficult. Not much has yet happened in this area. I believe we have a great deal of homework ahead of us before we really get going.

On the other hand, these traditional African churches reveal the challenge that mainline churches have not yet fully faced. They are actually very deeply rooted in the culture and in the life experience of the people to whom they appeal. So they put us to shame for being better and more deeply inculturated in Africa than we have been so far. When I say "we," I mean the mainline Christian churches. I certainly consider their appeal a challenge. We must examine this issue and ask ourselves what is really going on. That does not mean we question our faith, but we must question how we have been trying to root our faith in the cultural context. We must ask ourselves what makes such communities so attractive to our Christians.

The cardinals' consistory of 1991 dealt with the topic of sects and independent Christian communities. After lengthy consultation the cardinals decided, quite sensibly, not to condemn such communities out of hand. In fact, such communities have handed our Church a summons to a serious examination of why these groups and communities exercise such a strong attraction to our Christians in Africa. What do Christians find in such communities that is missing in the Church? Such sects or independent churches are not just a phenomenon in Africa, but are found all over the world. What must our churches do to have greater appeal for people in Africa — or in Asia or in America, for that matter? So in this sense I am saying that so-called "independent African churches" are sending us a message to which we must find an answer.

What is the status of dialogue with non-Christian traditional African faiths?

It has improved very much. Of course, we have not conducted great symposia, since the adherents of such traditional religions are not the kind of people who attend scholarly congresses. We emphasize a more pastoral approach toward the members of such traditional African religions. Concretely it means that Christians must try to learn more about such religions and understand better where they are coming from, so that after some examination they can determine which elements in these religions are good, worthwhile and positive. Possibly, the Church might even adopt some of these elements.

It would also become clear which elements should not be incorporated into Christianity. We have already spoken about that. In 1987 our office sent a pastoral letter to all the bishops' conferences of Africa, dealing with our contacts with the traditional religions of Africa. In the letter we indicated that these traditional religions provide a spiritual preparation and background for most of our Christians. We emphasized that they have consequently earned our respect and our careful study as well, so that they can become useful in our efforts at inculturation.

A few years later at a full assembly of our office we decided to send a similar letter to all the bishops in the world where there are traditional religions, such as the traditional religions of America and the ancestral religions of Asia and Australia. Everywhere bishops reported the same experience. As a rule, these traditional religions are very open and friendly to Christianity. For the most part, most new Christians come from these groups.

Do members of ancient non-Christian religions have a chance of salvation? It is hard to imagine that God only saves members of the Catholic Church. It is even harder to imagine that the salvation of billions of people depends on the human efforts of the churches and the success of their missionaries. Christ died and rose for all people. All, no matter when or where they live, are included in Christ's redemption.

You raise the whole great question of the relationship of non-Christian religions to salvation. . .

This question, which you call "great" is certainly less problematic theologically when it concerns the salvation of the individual person. But what significance do the non-Christian religions as a whole have in salvation history? In other words, what role do non-Christian religions play in the divine plan of salvation?

The Second Vatican Council spoke about that extensively in articles 13 to 17 of the constitution *Lumen gentium*. Article 13 emphasizes that all people are called into the unity of the People of God. They are in this unity already, or else they are related to it in some way or another. All Catholics, all who believe in Jesus Christ, all who believe in the one God, and everybody else, are called to salvation. This clearly comes about through the grace of God, which is the grace of Christ, the savior of all.

Of course, God desires the salvation of all. Paul already stated that in his letter to Timothy. Salvation and redemption have been accomplished in Jesus Christ. Article 15 of the constitution *Lumen gentium* develops these thoughts for non-Catholic Christians; article 16 expressly states that other people, such as Jews, Muslims, and Buddhists, are also included in God's plan of salvation.

The Second Vatican Council expressly said that all people are included in God's plan of salvation. If we add to that what we read in article 22 of *Gaudium et spes,* that Christ in his saving work has united himself with every human being, then we can trust that in his own way God has included everyone in the paschal mystery of salvation through the death and resurrection of Christ.

To return to your question, that means, all people can be saved. Of course, this presupposes that they are following their conscience and that they do not knowingly shut out God's grace, so that the grace just described in the words of the Council can reach them.

It would be futile to carry on long discussions about how and why God manifests his saving purpose in that way. We should not presume that we can figure out all the details. God can grant his grace as he wills with perfect freedom — even outside the visible confines of the Church.

We can certainly say that everyone who is saved is saved through the saving work of Christ. There is no other savior and redeemer. So they are connected to the Church as the continuation of the body of Christ, even if we do not know the exact nature of this connection or how to define it theologically. It is sufficient that we weak human beings accept that we are the family into which God sent his Son so that he might gather the dispersed and incorporate them into the family of God, the Church.

Without doubt elements that make people receptive to divine grace are present even in non-Christian religions. Thomas Aquinas states that it is entirely irrelevant who speaks a truth; we can elaborate his thought and trust that the Holy Spirit is at work — even in other people, religions and cultures besides our own. But only in the Church do we find the ordinary way to salvation and the fullness of saving grace.

Do non-Christian religions then play a role in God's saving plan?

One can draw that conclusion, but it is quite difficult to define that role. The mystery of salvation includes all people in a way that is ultimately known only to God. If people sincerely follow their conscience and dutifully

serve God according to the norms of their religion —
assuming that these norms do not embrace anything
fundamentally evil — then they can certainly share in the
saving work of Christ. This is true even if they do not
expressly recognize him as Savior and Redeemer. These
ideas certainly require further theological explanation
and precision. It is difficult to understand the role such
religions play in God's plan of salvation, but some positive elements in them cannot be denied.

*I am sure that you would agree that we are created as religious
beings. Given that aspect of our nature, does every person have to
follow his or her conscience to attain salvation? If I have under-
stood correctly that non-Christians must live conscientiously
according to their religion, then it ultimately follows that their
religion has a place in the divine plan of salvation.*

Yes, basically that is correct.

*Could non-Christian religions be defined as divinely willed
"preparatory conditioning for the Church"? The theologian Karl
Rahner spoke of "anonymous Christians," who are in the state of
grace but are unaware of it since they do not have the visible guarantee of the sacraments.*

I have reservations about putting people in categories,
although it may sometimes be legitimate to try. Let us be
content with saying simply that other religions play a role
in the divine plan and that they can be a help in attaining
salvation.

You see, thanks to divine providence, traditional
African religions have prepared the people of our region
for Christianity. Even if people may not have been knowingly aware, they had a deep desire for enlightenment.

But I would not want to say that all religions are equal here. For example, Judaism plays a special role. The Jewish people were God's first chosen, as we read throughout the Old Testament. There is no question that, along with their many positive aspects, religions include errors and some elements that are anything but holy. It would be a mistake to take my words as any kind of "canonization" of all religions. But without doubt, many religions contain elements that prepare people for salvation in Christ. Some religions do that better than others.

That is certainly a very respectful approach to other religions. But then, if we see things in that light, must we not formulate new descriptions? "Non-Christian" or "non-Christian religions" are rather unsatisfactory terms. Muslims or Hindus or Buddhists would not appreciate being described in terms of what they are not.

I agree. We would not like being described in negative terms, for example, as non-Muslims. A Muslim once asked me if I would like to be called a "non-Muslim." Naturally I said, "No, I would not like that." Then he asked, "Why then do you call us non-Christians?" We got the point. When our office was established in 1964 it was called the "Secretariat for Non-Christians." This could serve only as a working title. At that time we had a "Secretariat for Non-Believers," a "Secretariat for Non-Christians" and a "Secretariat for other Christians." That may have been very logical, but psychologically it was not very deferential to our partners. So in 1988 the pope renamed the office "The Pontifical Council for Interreligious Dialogue." The office itself did not change, but the name now conveys a more positive description of its work.

When something can be described in positive terms, it is generally better to do so.

To follow this line of thought, would it not be better to speak of a "Christian presence" or "Christian witness" rather than of "mission"? For believers of other religions, the Christian concept of "mission" has not only a positive aspect but — as a result of the history of the missions — a negative connotation.

I disagree with you here. The concept of "mission" comes directly from the commission of Jesus Christ. "Mission" means nothing other than "sending." In commissioning the Church, Christ was issuing a divine mandate. The biblical basis is clear. Jesus told his apostles, "As the Father has sent me, I also send you." Today we generally refer to this commissioning as evangelization. It means the same thing: the spread of the good news of Jesus Christ. They are equivalent concepts. Whether I speak of "mission" or of "evangelization" I mean the same thing. Your suggestion, "witness for Christ" conveys the same idea, if we understand "witness" in the fullest sense of the term.

I think that Muslims, for example, would not see it that way. They would be able to accept "Christian presence" or "Christian witness," but wouldn't "mission" sound like proselytizing, creating suspicion that the missionaries are attempting to lure believers away from Islam?

That is true if we limit mission solely to preaching. But mission and preaching are not exactly the same thing. Preaching is part of mission, not the whole of it. Interreligious dialogue is also a part of mission. Pope Paul VI expressly stated that. "Dialogue and Mission," a document formulated by our office in 1984, made the same point. As Pope John Paul II said in chapter 5 of *Redemptoris missio,* evangelization involves a whole list of words and actions: the witness of preaching, the quiet witness of a simple Christian presence, witness through social outreach to others, serving the sick and the poor, preaching Christian doctrine, catechizing, baptizing, organizing Christian communities and also the witness of interreligious dialogue. All these things together can be called the "mission of the Church." This mission is the very essence of the Church, and if you were to dispense with it, then you can say farewell to the original purpose of the Church.

So mission is as old as the Church itself. In some parts of the world, however, actual mission activity is quite recent — in some parts of Africa, your native continent, it began less than a century ago. May we talk about missionary methods? What is the role, for example, of the mission schools in Nigeria?

We should not underestimate the role the school has played in the development of the human person. Schools do much more than communicate cultural skills such as reading, writing and arithmetic, because the school enables people to participate in the entire inheritance of human-kind and then draw out implications for their own development. In Nigeria, the school provided the strongest impetus for the country's scientific, cultural and political development. Almost without exception, the politicians who led our country to independence are products of our mission schools. So naturally the school played a large role in the religious development of Nigeria.

*I*s *that typical only of Nigeria?*

It is true of all of Africa. Furthermore, I would say that without schools we would not have been able to rediscover and appreciate our own African traditions. Medical development and care for the sick would have been unthinkable if the schools had not prepared people for medical studies. In short, without the school there would have been no development.

Having said all that, I would not overlook the role the school played in evangelization; it was very significant. But that is not unique to Africa. All over the world Catholic schools are important instruments in proclaiming and deepening the faith. We should be proud that the Church organized the first schools in history. We can be proud that the first universities, even in Europe, were Church foundations — whether at Bologna, Oxford or Cologne. In the Middle Ages the Church was simply *the* "chief educator."

*W*e *have discussed the positive side of mission, but we should not overlook the dark side, the misguided development that occurred when Christianizing and Europeanizing went hand in hand. How do African bishops today feel about traditional missionary work as it was practiced in the recent history of the continent?*

The bishops of Africa hold differing opinions, and certainly history is open to various assessments. But they all do agree on one thing — and it not just they, but the priests, religious orders and laity as well: today we must do everything we can to bring the good news to people by the best means available. That is our goal, rather than trying to second-guess mistakes that missionaries made several hundred years ago.

In Africa, at least in the Church, we focus less on colonial problems from the past than on the concerns of today. We face pressing issues — social justice, for example, and how people of different ethnic backgrounds can live together harmoniously in national unity and respect for persons who hold other religious affiliations. Our chief concern is to develop Christian communities that live the gospel in a credible fashion. Our main tasks are cultivating good Christian families and establishing Christian principles in business and political life as well as overcoming new social problems, such as the breakup of marriages, abortion, and growing materialism.

Much more than past mistakes of missionaries, African bishops today are concerned about the training of religious professionals and the need to obtain more missionaries from outside Africa to serve the People of God in our continent. We do not want to be just a village church; we want to become a world Church. Missionaries from abroad are a clear sign of that. Exchange of personnel with the universal Church prevents offshoots that are not Catholic. Our Church is worldwide and that is why we want to share resources. You see, here in Italy alone there are twenty-six convents with Nigerian sisters. These sisters are not here for education or study but to give witness to the world Church. These are the issues, problems and responsibilities that our bishops are dealing with rather than wasting time on the distant past.

Cardinal Arinze, the demographics Nigeria has three large religious groupings: Christians, Muslims and members of traditional African religions. What was your experience of these religions as a young man at home? Did you have any contact with

*Muslims or with animists? What was it like in daily life? Was
there any dialogue, even in a limited way, between representatives
of different religions?*

When I was still a boy in school and later as a semi-
narian I had no contact with Muslims. There were no
Muslims living in my area of eastern Nigeria, but I did
have daily contact with believers of the traditional
African religions. There were many of them in my area
and most Christians came from this group. At that time
there was no organized dialogue. We lived together and
had daily personal contacts, which brought me early on to
study the religion of my people, the Igbos. I chose to write
my doctoral dissertation on the concept of sacrifice in the
traditional religion. I wanted this project to contribute to
explaining the sacrifice of the Mass in the familiar
thought patterns and conceptual categories of my people.

Muslims live in another part of Nigeria. Naturally,
Christians growing up there have contact with Muslims
from childhood on, as I had contact with adherents of our
traditional African religions. Today there are many efforts
to encourage Christians and Muslims to meet one
another. There are various forms of interreligious
dialogue; besides direct discussion of different religious
doctrines there is the indirect exchange over common
ethical, social and ecological issues. In Nigeria we find
that it is generally easier to practice indirect dialogue.

Many Muslims avoid direct interreligious dialogue
because they feel it makes truth relative, but they are
quite open to a so-called "cultural dialogue."

Psychologically, it is not useful to begin discussing
doctrine at the very first meeting with people of other religions; it is like barging right through the front door.

It is much wiser to begin with what we call "cultural dialogue." For example, first we speak about issues that concern the family or child rearing, topics such as youth and drug abuse, honorable behavior in public life, problems of corruption, or AIDS, a very urgent issue in Africa. We can speak about problems of different tribes living together harmoniously. We need to begin with issues such as those, which weigh heavily on people regardless of their religion.

Of course interreligious dialogue should not end there. When partners in such dialogue become well-acquainted, when they have established an atmosphere of trust, when they have learned to love one another — if I may use that lofty word — then they can address more difficult matters. For example, a group of scientists from North Africa and France have formed an organization known as the "Research Group for Christian-Islamic Issues." They also have dealt with religion and have published a book on the sacred scriptures of Christians and Muslims. A second publication dealt with Christian and Muslim views of justice. Unfortunately, dialogue rarely proceeds that far.

Clearly, dialogue should not begin with doctrine. Muslims are especially sensitive in that area,but Catholics too would not like to initiate dialogue with a difficult topic like the mystery of the Holy Trinity or the place of Mary as Mother of God or the role of Christ as unique savior. These central doctrines are not and should not be open to debate. One may eventually get to them in inter-religious dialogue, but that presumes really having come to accept one another, trust one another, and meet together in mutual love. When those conditions are met, and when partners in dialogue have established a broad basis of trust , then they are in a position to address such issues with some theological preparation. But other questions are more immediate — for example, our relationship with God, prayer, the duty to love our neighbor and the like. Nevertheless, dialogue should not begin even with these. There are more practical issues with which to start.

Christ in All
Cultures

Religious
Extremists and Intolerance

Today, even if Christians proceed in religious dialogue with an attitude of tolerance, one that proceeds from religious conviction rather than a demand for civil rights, we find that other religions do not always display the same attitude. On the contrary, a new fundamentalism in some religions is increasing even as tolerance is growing in others. All of this seems to make dialogue more difficult. There are, for example, fundamentalist tendencies within Islam. Even in Hinduism, a religion traditionally considered tolerant, fanaticism seems to be on the increase. Is significant interreligious dialogue even possible?

Extremist groups in many religions constitute a serious problem for interreligious dialogue. Some groups claim complete freedom to preach and to worship for themselves, even though they deny it to everyone else. Such a stance undermines the basis for dialogue, which must include respect for the rights of each partner. That goes for all matters of conscience and religion.

Those commonly known today as "fundamentalists" — I prefer the term "religious extremists" — are generally intolerant even within their own religion. They persecute fellow believers who do not share their particular form of religious practice. In their view, adherents of other religions have no rights whatever.

I grant that such people are deeply convinced of their position. But conviction is not the only necessary virtue. There is also an obligation for a certain objectivity, and this must include respect for the convictions of others. It is not just a matter of due tolerance, but a basic question of justice. Justice must uphold religious freedom. Tolerance is almost too negative a term. After all, you can even tolerate evil. On the contrary, respect is a positive attitude.

Religions themselves, thank God, are not responsible for such religious extremism. Only certain sects within Islam and Hinduism, at least until now, display growing intolerance and deny others the right to practice their religion. Such groups not only obstruct dialogue; they also restrain the leaders of their own faithful who approve of dialogue. Obviously religious dialogue receives no encouragement in such quarters; as a rule it is thoroughly resisted. That is a great disappointment. We can only hope that it will be possible to convince such people that no one is contesting their right to their own convictions, but they should at least concede the same right to others.

In a 1964 issue of L'Osservatore Romano *you characterized the foundation of the Vatican Secretariat for Non-Christians, today's Pontifical Council for Interreligious Dialogue, as a "visible sign" that the Catholic Church "reaches out to other*

*believers with open arms." Everyone must cooperate with the work
of dialogue "so that Christians and non-Christians can build
together a community of love." In the same paper Archbishop
Marcello Zago, then Secretary of the Council, criticized "Islam's
resistance to dialogue." He pointed out that in many Islamic
countries Christians have even been denied freedom of worship. In
1987 you also criticized an "expansive and aggressive Islam" at
the Roman bishops' synod, and as proof you referred to the situation in Sudan, Malaysia, and elsewhere. Today the list of such
countries is growing. Today, how real is that divide between openness to dialogue in the Catholic Church, but resistance within
Islam?*

Unfortunately resistance is a very real problem. Let me
try to answer by saying that through her Pontifical
Council for Interreligious Dialogue the Catholic Church
demonstrates that she would like to work together with
the faithful of other religions. We also want to show that
we are animated by the desire to see a guarantee of religious freedom for every human person. We desire the
cooperation of all people regardless of their religion.

Nevertheless, what Archbishop Zago wrote is true. He
mentioned one dimension; I addressed the other. I
pointed out that the Catholic Church stands for interreligious dialogue, and he emphasized that the Catholic
Church hopes Muslims will face this dialogue with openness. He expressed the hope that all religions, Muslims
and non-Muslim alike, would acknowledge freedom of
religion. We commit ourselves without reservation to religious freedom for Muslims in Catholic countries — Italy,
Spain or in mixed Christian countries such as Great
Britain and Germany — and likewise we expect that religious freedom will be granted Christians throughout the

Muslim world — whether it be Saudi Arabia, United Arab Emirates, Pakistan, Bangladesh, Egypt, Algeria or Libya.

We are convinced that the right to religious freedom is a human right that is binding everywhere. It is not a right given by the Church or the Mosque or any other authority; it comes directly from God. That is why it should be binding in every country. The pope has emphasized that again and again. In 1996, for example, at the inauguration of a big mosque in Rome, he said: "It is right for Muslims who live here to have a place to worship. On the same grounds it is also right and fair that Christians everywhere have the right to free practice of their religion."

In the West, Muslims do have a completely uncontested right to practice their religion freely. Unfortunately that is not true in Muslim countries such as Saudi Arabia or to a growing extent in a Hindu country such as India. This is true, even though organized interreligious dialogue is now in its fourth decade, a dialogue that includes representatives from those very countries.

True, but how do you propose to change that? Shall we call in the army? Of course not. We must work patiently toward the goal. We can only try to communicate and persuade. Naturally we address this issue on the political level too — for example, with the governments of Islamic countries who employ Christian workers. We point out that they have a duty to their own citizens to stand up for religious freedom. The Church continues to raise its voice loudly and clearly over this.

Are we supposed to defend this right, even when it is denied us?

Yes.

So predominantly Christian countries should allow the building of mosques even though there are no Christian churches in Muslim countries?

Members of other religions living in Christian countries have a right to obtain land from government authorities for building a gathering place for worship. In this case there is no question of the "lex talionis," "an eye for an eye, a tooth for a tooth." We can only reiterate that Muslims, Hindus and Buddhists have religious freedom in Germany, Spain or Finland, and so we expect full religious freedom for Christians in countries where other believers are the majority, whether it be Saudi Arabia, Thailand or India.

We cannot turn the tables, saying, you do not give Christians religious freedom, so we will close the mosques or temples in our country. Granting religious freedom is not a sign of weakness but of preeminent strength. We must not shrink from interceding everywhere, with every appropriate means at our disposal, for the universal right to religious freedom. The Church cannot do it alone; she needs the support of the government. Unfortunately many administrations in Christian countries of Europe fail to support this right of their citizens in non-Christian countries with due emphasis.

You have spoken at some length about human rights. Does this term have the same meaning in all cultures? Let me give an example. In 1989 a high-level Vatican delegation under your direction held a conference in Tripoli, led by the general secretary of the "World Islamic Call Society," Muhammad Ahmed Sharif. At its conclusion, the conference issued a declaration that both religions had a fundamental interest in the advancement of

*peace and human rights. Given that the conference occurred in the
capital of Libya, I wonder whether both sides meant the same
thing when they spoke of peace and human rights.*

I have my doubts about that too. In meetings like that
we must always make an effort to define clearly what such
terms really mean. If that is not done, then each side inter-
prets it their own way. But even with such efforts, there is
no guarantee that concepts shaped by different cultures
and history really have the same meaning.

For Christians, concepts like peace, freedom and
justice may have different implications than they have for
Muslims. That gets into very practical questions
regarding the administration of justice. If, according to
the norms of Sharia, a thief has a hand cut off many
Muslims consider that an expression of practical justice.
For Christians such punishment violates basic human
rights.

Or consider the concept of religious freedom. For
Christians religious freedom means that all human beings
have the right to practice their religious convictions
freely. For some Muslims, however, religious freedom
means that every human being has the right to convert to
Islam.

Conversion to Islam is viewed as a God-pleasing act,
while abandoning Islam and converting to another religion for reasons of conscience is considered a capital
crime.

This is an example of how the same word, "conversion,"
can have very different meanings.

But I must also point out that participants in interreligious dialogue are not the rulers of the country from
which they come. It often happens that our dialogue part-

ners are aware of the defects in their societies and they address them, but do not have the power to change political conditions. That is also true on the Christian side of the dialogue. We also lack the political means to change goals like religious freedom in keeping with our own views.

The man you identified as general secretary of the "World Islamic Call Society," Dr. Sharif, I regard as an honorable person. He sees many deficiencies in his country but, in fairness to him, he does not have the power to change them. When Dr. Sharif agrees with a certain principle we work out together in such a dialogue, he does not hesitate to agree strongly with it.

Reaching agreement, of course, does not automatically change the situation, but it sends out messages that carry a strong signal.

Together with the Pontifical Council, you stand for tolerance, cooperation and love among members of different religions. Does it pain you to see the rise of religious extremism rather than tolerance among various religions and in many countries? In the last few years the Church has even experienced martyrdom. I am thinking of the killing of missionaries in Algeria.

Of course that is very sad. You mention Algeria. At that time the Holy Father sent me to Algeria to celebrate a requiem Mass for the murdered missionaries. Seven monks had been murdered. But just before the burial, as you may remember, the retired archbishop of Algiers, Cardinal Leon Duval, who had personally founded the monastery of the murdered monks, also died. His coffin was placed alongside those of the murdered Trappists. Naturally that was a very painful time.

But it is also worth mentioning that — in spite of these orgies of hate — the relationship between the great majority of people, that is, between Muslims and the small number of Christians who continue to persevere, has become more understanding and friendly. Regard for the Christian minority has grown because the Muslim majority realizes that Christians are ready to risk their lives. As a result, Muslims have extended real love and respect to their Christian neighbors.

Given all the confusion over the situation in Algeria, it would be inappropriate to interpret the controversy as a Christian-Muslim war. By far the greatest number of victims of this religious extremism are Muslims. So it is a matter of an inter-Islamic conflict based on political and economic issues, not primarily a campaign against Christians. The plight of Algeria is nationwide and not limited to the small Christian community. I would also like to point out that Islamic dignitaries have condemned the crimes of the Algerian fanatics as strongly as we have.

So we know that this act does not reveal one religion pitted against another, but unruly adherents of one religion acting against their own brethren as well as against those of a different faith. Here I can only cite the Holy Father who again emphasized that violence is foreign to every religion — and I think most Muslims would agree with this too. No real religion can proclaim violence in God's name. The extent to which members of a religion make violence a religious precept reveals what poor members of that faith they are. Despite all its anguish, our experience in Algeria will not lead us to falter or surrender. Our Christian witness in Algeria will remain uncompromised for the future.

Excuse me if I pose a provocative question. Do you feel closer to a faithful Muslim than to a liberal-minded business executive, who in some way has been influenced by the Christian tradition, but no longer considers the gospel relevant to his daily life?

In interreligious dialogue it is always preferable to deal with people who are really filled with their faith — whether they be Christian, Muslim, Hindu or Buddhist. Those who live their faith are always more suitable as partners in dialogue than those for whom faith no longer constitutes an important component of their lives. However I do not want to make an artificial comparison by saying that a good Muslim is better than a poor Christian. One should not compare the best of one religion with the worst of another. That would be an oversimplification. Every religion has members who are sincere in living their faith and others for whom their faith means little. Each person's real situation — that, I think, we must leave to God.

The most fruitful dialogue would seem possible between Christians and Jews. Despite all political burdens of anti-semitism and the terrible sufferings of the Jewish people, at least they acknowledge a common heritage, in Martin Buber's words "one book and one hope." They share a common point of departure.

That is certainly true. What we call the Old Testament for the Jews is simply the Bible.

That alone tells us that Christians and Jews have a sizeable common heritage. Pope John Paul II rightly called the Jews "our elder brothers." We Christians should not forget that our savior Jesus Christ was Jewish. His mother Mary was Jewish, as were the apostles. In the beginning, Christianity was considered a Jewish sect. Given such a common background, the relationship between Christians and Jews should be characterized by deep friendship. We must not forget that the promises God made to Abraham and his descendants were never withdrawn. Realizing this places a great duty on us as Christians.

At the same time, one of the most delicate issues in the Christian-Jewish dialogue is that of "mission." Jews reject Christian mission endeavors. Does the Catholic understanding of mission, which you described as essential to the faith, allow for some exception?

If I am convinced that God sent his only-begotten Son into the world to save us, and that this redeeming work of his cross and resurrection happened for each and every one of us, then there can be no exceptions. How can I withhold this Good News, this great hope from others? Sharing this message of hope and assurance of salvation is nothing other than a form of loving others.

Yet, religion is always something to be proposed, never imposed. We would not and must not spread the Good News by pressure or force in any shape or form. Political, economic or social pressure as a means of evangelization is not only inappropriate, it is entirely unacceptable. That would be a form of proselytism, which no one accepts today. But if we are free to proclaim our faith, and others are free to hear it and free to accept it or not, then exercising such a human right cannot be unacceptable. Of course, these principles are true for people on both sides of the confessional divide.

If anyone wishes to accept Christ, no one should stand in the way. The Second Vatican Council said as much in the document *Dignitatis humanae*. The Church can never renounce sharing the Good News with everyone. A

Church that would renounce that mission would relegate itself to a deep freezer or the Vatican museum. Saint Paul said, "The love of Christ urges us on." Our faith demands that we reach out to all, at least to those who are open and willing. Besides, all have the right to hear the good news if they want to.

Not a One-World Religion

Do goals like the encouragement of peaceful co-existence among members of different religions, development, civic virtue and the struggle for justice and peace provide an adequate basis for a common effort among members of different faiths? What is the goal of interreligious dialogue?

All the areas you mentioned are partial goals of interreligious dialogue. But they do not complete the whole picture, nor do they reveal the ultimate goal. In interreligious dialogue, members of different religions meet on the level of the spirit, expecting that such meetings will bear fruit. This fruit may be the rediscovery of the wealth of one's own religion, which may lead to mutual encouragement in our search for God.

Human solidarity, peace among nations, ecology and greater equality among the rich and the poor — these are certainly important for humankind. But for people of faith they are not enough. For us, the highest goal is knowing and serving God and finally arriving in his presence. Interreligious dialogue ultimately will help the participants to achieve that.

It can be helpful if we try to see ourselves through the eyes of others. When others put into words how they view me, that can lead to real self-knowledge. It can help me, for example, recognize where I have been less than faithful to my religious heritage. Mahatma Gandhi put it very clearly when he said, "I love Christ, but so few Christians follow his teaching." His statement challenges us to keep the purpose of religious dialogue always clearly in view. Interreligious dialogue also builds community by promoting harmony in society. It contributes to love for one another. These goals reach far beyond practical results, which are goals too, but only partial ones.

So the goal is not some kind of world religion?

Oh no, certainly not. It would be a complete misunderstanding to think of interreligious dialogue as a blender, that you toss various ingredients into — in this case, religions. Then, when you whip them all together, out would come something entirely new — a "one-world religion." No, we are not talking about a "religious blender." That would be nothing but religious syncretism.

Naturally as a cardinal of the Roman Catholic Church I would be happy if everyone in the world shared my faith. Then the Holy Father could dissolve the Council for Interreligious Dialogue. But we really have no "secret strategy" in our dialogue. I must honestly and emphatically say that we are not concocting schemes to bring our dialogue partners in as converts through the back door. Of course, conversion could occur if a Christian presents a convincing witness for Christ. Partners in religious dialogue should always be open to the leading of the Spirit, to accept the faith, but we do not prescribe this.

We are not like those who ask flippantly, "What is truth?" and then, like Pilate, refuse to wait for the answer. Pilate, if I may add, is the model for all those who irresponsibly ask about truth with a shrug of their shoulders, and then avoid the answer. They avoid it because they fear it. Partners in religious dialogue need not fear the truth. The goal of dialogue is not to convince a partner of the truth of my religion through pressure, scheming or any such means. Even if Muslims tell me, "We are Muslims and have no interest at all in becoming Christian," they can still be my partners in dialogue. Dialogue with them still makes perfect sense. Again, the goal of dialogue is the meeting; it is mutual enrichment, cooperation, openness to God's action, growth in one's own faith. Any further possibilities we confidently leave to divine providence. Spreading the faith by force or pressure is foreign to dialogue and inconsistent with human dignity. Yet everyone has the duty before God to seek religious truth and, when found, to follow it.

I would like turn our conversation to the concept of a "world ethic." Do you think there is a common ethical core in all religions?

At the center of the human heart or soul, however you say it, there certainly is a fundamental precondition for religion. It is here, for example, that we find a general acknowledgment of God as the ground of all being to whom we owe recognition, thanks and service. Every human heart is stamped with an outline of a code of conduct toward others. In this sense we may speak of elements common to all religions.

In the philosophical sense, an ethic governing daily life can be found in every religion. These philosophical principles can bridge the cultural differences in communicating the basic ground rules for human relationships. Take, for example, the awareness that life has value, or that I cannot simply appropriate for myself the property of others, or that those to whom I owe my life, my mother and father, have a claim to my love and respect. The various religions do not disagree over these things. You could also say that, to a great extent, the content of the Ten Commandments reflects the common heritage of all religions. But I think there is more to be said. Religion offers us more than these basic similarities. At times of moral crisis philosophy alone does not take us far enough. We look to religion for concrete ways to shape our lives. For us Christians the moral law is an integral part of our religion, our life in Christ. Ours is not just some kind of free-floating philosophy.

You have touched on key concepts in the dialogue: no syncretism on the one side or proselytizing on the other. Is it incorrect, then, to maintain that evangelization means helping a Muslim to become a better Muslim and helping a Hindu to become a better Hindu? Some Christian theologians hold that position.

That clearly contradicts what we have described as the mission mandate of Jesus Christ, which is binding on his Church. Sharing the Good News of the gospel with everyone — that is what we mean when we speak of our mission as Christians — is the enduring task of the Church. The witness of the apostles is quite clear, and we stand by this tradition today.

Our Catholic faith has never embraced the idea that we are just one religion among many and that therefore it makes no difference whether we proclaim our faith or not. No, the duty to proclaim the good news of redemption through Jesus Christ remains valid for all time. In December, 1990, Pope John Paul II emphasized this in his encyclical *Redemptoris missio.* Saint Paul warns us, "Woe to me if I do not preach the gospel!" Evangelization should not be confused with proselytizing. Proselytizing involves improper and unworthy methods of conversion and is to be condemned. Evangelization, on the other hand, means proclaiming the gospel of Jesus Christ in a worthy manner that respects human freedom. This is a duty.

In recent decades, Christians and non-Christians alike have become more aware of their responsibility towards creation and the environment. Some critics claim that Christianity is responsible for many ecological problems through the excessive influence of the biblical passage, "Fill the earth and subdue it." In contrast, most nature religions, such as those of native North Americans or the Asian religions, have been more sensitive and respectful toward the environment. How would you respond to such allegations?

Such a criticism certainly challenges Christians. But we need to analyze that passage more carefully. The verse, "Fill the earth and subdue it," comes from Genesis, the first book of the Bible. It contains God's command to our first parents. I understand this sentence to mean that God entrusted to humans the care of visible creation on his behalf. God indeed places us as stewards over his entire creation. But that includes taking responsibility for creation. So it would be entirely false to assume that human beings can exercise unrestricted and arbitrary rule over creation. God is and remains Lord of creation. Hence Christianity must repudiate every irresponsible attitude toward creation, and the biblical mandate supports that.

On the other hand you are entirely right when you credit certain nature religions, to which I would add Shintoism in Japan, with an especially gentle, responsible and benign attitude toward nature. Certainly, in Christian cultures responsibility for creation has never been taken as seriously as today. On the other hand — and that is the flip side of the coin — nowhere have the natural sciences taken the verse "Subdue the earth" so seriously as they have in Christian cultures.

This has had a two-fold effect. On the one hand insights from the natural sciences have led to greater responsibility for creation, but on the other science has increased the danger. Let me offer an example. The development of bigger and faster airplanes has required longer and wider runways. That requires the expansion of airports, which always poses environmental problems. Planes pollute the air with noise and exhaust. So improvement in human communication comes at a high price.

Our great task today is to harmonize progress with conservation as much as possible, preserving respect for God's creation. Christians must ensure that in our own lifetimes we do not ruin the good things that God in his goodness has given us. More than ever, technical progress requires ethical regulation more than ever. Many religions see that very clearly, but in our generation a sense of responsibility for creation and the environment also has grown among Christians. We should not forget the example of Francis of Assisi, who had a very high respect for nature.

Pope John Paul II is a fervent proponent of such efforts. He pointed out that these concerns are a part of our faith and that we should confront them as Christians. We can never say: that is not our problem; that is the business of the world, not the Church. We are not masters of God's creation but stewards, with a great responsibility to future generations. Ruining creation would be a grave injustice toward our descendants — and a violation of one of the cardinal virtues.

Religious extremists and even some moderates do not share your positive attitude toward interreligious dialogue. Some Catholics see danger in interreligious dialogue. They reason that engaging with people of other faiths can put their own faith in danger, especially if the other religions present attractive qualities. How would you respond to such concerns?

I never said that contact with other religions is without danger, especially for those not well rooted in their own faith. Those who know their faith and have a positive relationship with the heritage of their Church or religion, and who in difficult situations can turn to the help and counsel of serious theologians, run a very slight risk. Those who have only vague ideas about their religion and faith can easily be shaken when confronted by the claims of other religions. Those who can't swim shouldn't dare into deep water.

Would you say, then, that interreligious dialogue on the theological level assumes a good deal of knowledge and competence in one's own faith and cannot be carried on by "ordinary" members of each faith, since these are in danger of all too easily being theologically "run over"?

If you are speaking about the discussion of fundamental faith issues, only those who are intellectually and theologically capable of this should engage in it. But we have also spoken of many other forms of dialogue, especially the dialogue of daily life, in which people of different religions meet in everyday situations. These encounters entail no discussion of dogma, only an amicable sharing of life. If someone gets involved with the poor, the needy, or with drought or flood victims, the hungry and sick, this kind of everyday dialogue of life holds no dangers that I can see. Still, I would not recommend that those the necessary qualifications engage in discussions that touch on the basis of one's religion. Such discussion could in fact lead to danger.

Others disagree with interreligious dialogue because close dealings with those from other faith convictions could lead to indifferentism or relativism.

That can happen if partners in such a dialogue are not adequately prepared. If they are not well-grounded in their own religion and in living their faith, they can end up in indifferentism. But here again what I have just said is true: if they are really grounded in their faith and love their church or faith community, there is little danger of relativism.

Your last two questions seem to reflect the prevailing popular notion that interreligious dialogue should be left to philosophers and theologians. I would like to emphasize again that this is only one area of interreligious dialogue and perhaps not the most important. I have participated in many meetings with religious leaders in which we say hardly a word about dogmatic issues. For example, when, as has often happened, a group of Shinto leaders visited me to tell me how much they esteem the pope, I then told them with deep feeling how I had visited their shrines in Japan and learned much about them. As a consequence, we established mutual respect and esteem for each other's belief systems. We departed with the awareness that we had made progress in brotherhood and both sides had set an example for their own faithful. That, too, is a form of dialogue, even if it is different from a lofty theological or intellectual discourse. Building trust between religions is a gesture of great value.

You see, such gestures are possible for everyone. Even very simple people can do that — whether they are Christian, Muslim, Buddhist or Hindu. In reality it usually comes off quite well. When Christians and Muslims in my country meet, it is almost always over practical issues of helping fellow human beings. No one feels threatened by the other, or that one's religious identity is under fire. But once again: I urge discretion. I would not, for example, recommend that a Christian engage in Buddhist meditation without preparation. As a rule the average Christian knows far too little about Buddhism and even about Christian mysticism to gain from such an exercise, and it may harm them.

I'd like to explore this point further. In the Catholic Church — at least in western Europe — there is concern that young people are adopting the attractive aspects of far Eastern religions, such as lifestyle and meditation practices, without understanding the theological implications of their actions. As a result, they are distancing themselves from their own Church or even losing their faith.

That is a real concern. Unfortunately, many young people have not really learned how to pray, in the sense of meditative prayer of the heart. For many Christians prayer is restricted to the recitation of prayer texts. That is a valid form of prayer, but it is not the same as speaking with God in the depth of one's heart. Many young Christians simply have not learned how to do that. I don't want to start assigning blame by asking whether that is the fault of parents or maybe even of priests.

The fact is: this loss is regrettable. If people have not mastered contemplative prayer, it can be very dangerous to venture into the very different world of Buddhist meditation, which is not even directed toward God and in the strict sense cannot even be called prayer. A classic Buddhist does not pray but rather seeks greater self-awareness. Christian prayer strives for union with God; Buddhist meditation seeks interior freedom.

I would not hold it against any young Christian for going to Asia to seek enlightenment with the help of a guru. Instead, I would ask a self-critical question: where has Christianity failed? What are we missing that leaves young people unable to find what they need? What are religious orders, our monks and nuns, doing to help young people in their search for spiritual values? They certainly have the means! Every young person who goes to Asia to find enlightenment touches a painful wound, left by our shortcomings in spiritual formation by our failure to teach young people about prayer, asceticism, meditation and pondering the wonderful mysteries of our faith. Don't misunderstand me. I am not criticizing the rosary or the recitation of prayers that have been left to us by great people of prayer. We should hold on to our traditions. Nothing can replace personal prayer, conversing with God in the depths of one's heart.

Many Christians fear that entering into interreligious dialogue may lead to loss of faith, relativism, syncretism, or drifting into other religions and cults; I would include indifferentism as well, the feeling that one religion is as good as another . . .

That would be a serious theological error. It is a mistake to think that as long as you act morally it makes no difference what religion you profess.

If God sent into the world his Son, who said, "I am the way, the truth and the life," then the way is already established, and I cannot claim that every road leads me to salvation. Whether a Jew or a Muslim finds the way to salvation we must leave to God. Muslims who are sincere and live their faith and are convinced in their heart that their way corresponds to God's call can find salvation under certain conditions, as described in *Lumen gentium* (#16) and in *Dialogue and Proclamation* (#29). But that is always accomplished through the grace of Christ, the one and only savior. Religious indifferentism and religious relativism are very dangerous, fundamental errors. The best defense against them is to know the Christian religion and to love this faith. When Christians meet members of other religions, they do so as members and representatives of our faith community, our Church.

You have made clear the dangers that many see in interreligious dialogue. However, wouldn't it be a good idea to also discuss what it presupposes? The word "dialogue" implies that there are

*different positions. Where there is complete unity, dialogue would
be superfluous.*

That makes sense. Where there are no religious differences, there is religious unity. Where there is only one religion, naturally there is no interreligious dialogue. Perhaps an "intrareligious" dialogue could take its place. That would be like a Dominican and a Franciscan within the Catholic Church discussing the spiritual characteristics of their orders. There are many legitimate differences. Dominic was not a photocopy of Francis or Ignatius or Benedict.

*My question is really directed to a different matter. It seems that
interreligious dialogue assumes our willingness to preserve the
identity of our dialogue partner.*

We respect the identity of every participant in dialogue. Dialogue presumes this respect. As I said earlier, one participant converting another can never be a hidden agenda in dialogue. As long as there are people who hold religious convictions that differ from one another, there is a place for interreligious dialogue. As a Christian I naturally would be happy to see all people believe in Christ. My respect for non-Christian convictions, does not necessarily exclude my desire that others become Christian too.

*What if a "Dialogue of Life," the name you gave to one of the
forms of dialogue, leads to common prayer? Many traditional
Catholics' outlook were uncomfortable with the prayer meeting at
Assisi, for example, even though the Holy Father initiated it.
Common prayer or other signs of unity such as similar liturgical
vestments can be well intentioned, but they can also lead to confu-*

sion. Is it correct to share common prayer? What boundaries should we acknowledge?

Interreligious dialogue and common prayer are two separate matters. Interreligious dialogue does not include common prayer. Such interfaith worship would raise a number of serious issues.

Let me clarify some things about the prayer gathering in Assisi. The Holy Father did not in any way invite leading figures of different religions to common prayer, even if the opposite assertion is often made. There was, in fact, no common prayer at Assisi. The pope did invite representatives of different religions to fast and pray for peace, but to do it on their own. Each religion had its own place for prayer in Assisi.

Those who did pray together were Christians of various denominations, that is, Catholics, Orthodox, Anglicans, Presbyterians, Lutherans; all of them prayed together in the cathedral. They used a previously-agreed-upon ecumenical prayer of petition.

Prayer always flows from one's faith. To the degree that we agree in faith we can pray together. That is the situation among the various groups of Christians. But even here there are always certain painful limitations that result in different prayer styles. Again, Christians never held any kind of common adoration or worship with Muslims, Jews, Hindus or other great world religions. This is why neither here nor in other similar situations did the question of common liturgical vestments ever arise.

I want to tell you what occasionally happens at interreligious gatherings. The respective chairperson may ask a participant to offer a prayer right before the opening of the session. If for example a Muslim says, "May God be with us, may God lead and guide us, may God enlighten us and lead us to unity of thought and action," one can hardly raise an objection. All the other participants could say the same thing. But such a prayer is not in any way a formal prayer or worship service that would cause confusion.

The only people who raise objections to the prayer gathering at Assisi are those who were falsely informed about it or who have grossly misunderstood what it was all about. Naturally many Catholics were surprised that the pope agreed to invite leaders of other religions to Assisi and then sat down in their midst. But the pope does not apologize for that. He is convinced that all true prayer is inspired by the Spirit of God. Let me reiterate what that means. Not every prayer is inspired by the Holy Spirit, but every authentic, genuine prayer. To be present at such prayer and to listen to such prayer respectfully is not engaging in mixed worship or in interfaith worship. For example, when I see a Muslim pray, I respect that, even if it is a form of prayer that I find unfamiliar. At the closing event in the plaza in front of the basilica in Assisi a few members of the religions represented there prayed for a few minutes, while others listened with respectful attention. That is all it was. Those who criticize Assisi need to take note of that.

The Holy Father actually brought only one message to Assisi: if we wish to assure peace, we cannot leave religion out of the picture. The United Nations and governments with their foreign policy clearly cannot do it alone. The religious factor is undeniable. Since prayer is an essential expression of all religions, it was time for the various religions to make their desire for peace visible to the world by all coming together at one location to pray for peace.

How far can one go in attending feasts and celebrations of a religion different from one's own? Practically speaking, is it in keeping with dialogue or would it entail confusion for Christians to invite Muslims to celebrate their Id Al-Fitr in Christian cathedrals, or for Christian clergy to participate in Yom Kippur with Jews or in Mah-Schiva-Ratri with Hindus? If they do so, to what extent should they be involved? To what extent may representatives of other religions participate in Christian feasts?

Good will in contact with other religions can only be commended; nevertheless, it is crucial that different religions maintain their distinctive identity. One should be careful that the rites of another religion do not result in compromise or risk that one's identity becomes blurred.

When Muslims celebrate Id-Al-Fitr, it is better to arrange for the celebration in their own mosques. After the worship service of Id-Al-Fitr it is customary to hold a large banquet. If Christians are invited to this dinner, they should accept. I would see that as a sign of good will toward Muslims. But I would strongly discourage inviting Muslims to celebrate their religious feasts in Christian churches. Nor would I recommend this when Buddhists or Hindus or other religions are involved. Each religion should worship in its own house of worship.

Now, you may ask what members of other religions should do in the diaspora when they do not have their own house of worship? In such situations I would recommend that Christians, for example, could help Jews, Muslims, or Hindus rent a room or a hall. But, as I already said, I would strongly discourage making Christian churches available for such occasions. This is a question of Christian identity. I realize that good will lies behind such action, yet I consider it ill-advised.

That goes for the other way around as well. We should be very careful about inviting the faithful of other religions to the eucharist, for example. Eucharist is the central expression of our faith. Holy Mass is not an interfaith service; it is the highest form of Catholic worship. We would certainly not refuse an individual member of another religion who wants to attend a Mass. But one is obliged, I would say, to explain what goes on there. They should know that it is more than just a pious exercise; it concerns the core of the Christian faith.

Would you discourage members of different religions from praying together?

It is really better when each religion conducts its own worship and prays in its own fashion. Bringing together faithful from three or four religions for common prayer is theologically risky. Personally, I would not engage in that. I do not consider it a proper form of interreligious dialogue.

It is a different matter when at the beginning of an interreligious discussion one participant offers a short simple prayer which is in no way unsettling because it contains elements that everyone shares. Naturally, I consider something like that acceptable. But that is basically different from a formal prayer service performed by representatives of different religions.

You see, it is really quite obvious. How in conscience can a Muslim respond to a Christian Trinitarian prayer? Christians begin prayer as a rule with a Trinitarian sign of the cross.

Everyone should concern themselves with assuring that each religion can freely exercise its right to pray according to its own character without losing its distinct identity. Otherwise you only send out false signals that could give an impression to those who are not theologically astute that all religions are more or less the same and that differences no longer matter. That would be sending an entirely false signal with regard to interreligious dialogue.

Let me ask about another example of where to draw the line. What would you do if at a common gathering for interreligious dialogue a Muslim or Hindu, for example, were to come to a Catholic Mass and approach the altar to receive communion?

The Church lays down conditions for reception of the eucharist even for Catholics. If they have sinned seriously, even Catholics cannot come up to the Lord's Table, unless they first have received the sacrament of reconciliation. That is the first point. Secondly, eucharist presumes unity and agreement in faith, as well as unity with the bishops and the pope. That is why the eucharist is never appropriate as an interreligious celebration. So the answer is clear: only Catholics who have fulfilled the above conditions can receive communion. You know how problematic this issue is for separated Christians. For Muslims, Jews, Buddhists, Hindus or others the reception of communion is simply not possible.

Naturally, the place to begin the discussion is not at the communion rail, when the celebrant notices that a non-Christian wants to receive the body of the Lord. If you expect something like this might happen, then you should hold such a discussion before Mass. You have to be clear, naturally, but cordial. Without giving offense, you must explain that the eucharistic celebration is not some kind of friendship meal, but rather the very heart of Catholic worship. Similarly, a Catholic cannot take any kind of active role in the religious worship of another religion. That is also out of order.

I must emphasize it again: Catholics can play no active part in the worship of another religion. Naturally it is appropriate to attend a funeral or wedding of another religion. But to participate actively on either side is not interreligious dialogue but an act of theological confusion. In my experience, religions generally respect each other's need to preserve its own character.

For example, we participated in a large four-day dialogue meeting in Taiwan. It was held in a monastery with eight hundred Buddhist nuns and two hundred Buddhist monks. I asked the head of the monastic community if he could provide a place for us to celebrate Holy Mass. He did it readily with great cordiality. All four mornings, during the entire symposium, we celebrated Mass and then set out the Blessed Sacrament for adoration during the day.

Who are the representatives of other religions that you meet with? You yourself have a clear mandate: at the pope's request you represent the Catholic Church. With what authority or with whose mandate do Muslims, Buddhists, Hindus or Shintoists take part?

That is a good question, but it is a complicated issue. When we participate in interreligious dialogue it often becomes clear to us that the other religions have no organizational structure comparable to ours. For us it is clear who can represent and speak for the Church. When we meet with other religions they quickly notice the difference.

If I meet Buddhists from Japan or Thailand, or Muslims from Syria or Jordan, I know that my dialogue partners cannot speak for all Buddhists or for all Muslims. They are aware of that too. There are many institutions that can speak with special authority — for example, the Al-Azhar in Cairo speaks with a high measure of moral authority in the Muslim world. But even the Al-Azhar has no actual jurisdiction over all Muslims, as the pope has over all Catholics.

So they speak only for themselves?

No, that would put it too narrowly. They speak not only for themselves but also for a group of colleagues, though not for all their fellow believers. For example, the Islamic World Congress or the Muslim World League, are alliances whose leaders speak for their members, but only for their *own* members.

We have a committee for dialogue with Al-Azhar that meets once a year. With all these groups it is clear on both sides that they do not speak for all of the world's Muslims. Therefore these meetings never end with communiques that claim universal authority, but only with statements agreed upon by the participants at that dialogue. We are careful at such meetings not to claim more authority than is really there.

How far do you think that organizations of people from different world religions, such as the World Conference of Religions for Peace (WCRP), can help promote religious freedom in areas where it does not yet exist?

Such organizations can play a positive role. This role will certainly not be the same everywhere. The results will also depend on the people who get involved. They must be both competent and reliable. The World Conference of Religions for Peace is an undertaking of Muslims, Buddhists, Shintoists, Christians and others united in an honest and earnest effort to promote justice and to fight against discrimination of any kind. Today the WCRP is respected and recognized by the United Nations as a non-governmental agency. In the Pontifical Council for Interreligious Dialogue we have quite a favorable impression of this organization.

But who do the delegates to the WCRP really represent? Do Christian members of this conference speak with authority for their church? Do Muslims speak for Islam, and if so, for which Islam? How effective can such an organization be?

Half a loaf is better than none. Perfectionism can sometimes be the enemy of the good. One cannot always have perfection, and if one cannot accomplish the best, there still can be progress if one at least achieves second best.

Of course, the best, the ideal thing, would be to have official and fully authorized representatives of all religions at one table. But you can see how difficult that is even among Christian churches. It is easy for the Roman Catholic Church to appoint an authorized representative who can speak in the name of the universal Church or of a diocese. But you see how difficult that would be, for example, for the Orthodox or the Anglicans or the Protestant churches.

For Jews, Muslims, Buddhists or Hindus it is entirely unthinkable to have an authorized representative who can speak for all the faithful. Since that is not possible, we have to be content that it is still possible to have an organization like the WCRP bringing together faithful of different religions, who gather without any hierarchical mandate yet as individual persons have faced many issues and taken responsibility for peace and justice. A great many positive results have come from that.

Besides sometimes it is better that the faithful not always appeal to the highest authority but take personal responsibility themselves. Catholics who work for peace and justice do not need a papal appointment. They only need to appeal to their own conscience and sense of responsibility. The freedom of the children of God calls for just that kind of responsible personal initiative.

The Fruits of Steadfastness

Let's talk once more about the fruits of dialogue. What results do you see in the last four decades from this new contact the Catholic Church is making with the faithful of other religions?

My personal experience has been encouraging and positive. First of all it is worth noting that after forty years of interreligious dialogue many world religions communicate with one another regularly. Until recently that was not happening. We are ready to listen to one another. We begin by trying to understand one another. To use a biblical image, for a long time now the walls of Jericho have remained standing, but by taking away a few stones (our prejudices) the walls have become less of a barrier than they were forty years ago.

Many people of good will — certainly more in some parts of the world than in others — have become active in bringing members of different religions together in conversation on the local level. Positive developments do not appear spectacular, because they have taken place in everyday life on the local level. Every little positive effort that we have made together has encouraged us to go further. On the local level, prejudices have been overcome and on the theological level the dialogue has had gratifying results.

One example of the technological exchange with other religions on an academic level is the Pontifical Institute for Islamic and Arabic Studies here in Rome. This institute is directed by the Missionaries of Africa, the White Fathers. Those who attend it can earn a graduate degree. All of this is a fruit of the last forty years of dialogue. If such a pontifical institute is not a sign of high respect, even love, for our Muslim brothers and sisters, then I do not know what would better embody it. There are many such institutes.

On the local level, the practical results of forty years of the "new contact," as you say, of the Catholic Church with non-Christian religions in interreligious dialogue are almost too numerous to count. We are still a long way from solving all the problems with their deep religious roots. But we are certainly moving in the right direction.

These fruits, particularly in real life situations, show that interreligious dialogue has gone far beyond mere academic debate. If Catholics and Muslims operate a leper hospital without exchanging one word on dogmatic questions, but day by day do their job out of love for the sick and for one another, that is certainly a fruit of the new relationship you are asking about. Or take a very different example: in Pakistan, Christians and Muslims demonstrated together against the registering of religious affiliation on passports, because they know it could result in discrimination. That is also a sign of the new contact they have with one another. Christians and Muslims in Great Britain have demonstrated to protect the lives of the unborn. Recently in Sierra Leone, after terrible years of civil war, the national Christian-Muslim council brought the parties together again, thereby helping restore peace. Those examples show that interreligious dialogue is not just a theoretical matter, but bears practical fruit. I could continue listing examples for hours. It is true that a false understanding of interreligious dialogue has led some Christians to become negligent about proclaiming Christ to others. That attitude has led to religious indifferentism or relativism or syncretism. But we have already answered those concerns.

Obviously, you see no alternative to interreligious dialogue. However, such dialogue requires a great change of awareness, even among Catholics. Along with the willingness to reach out to others, it requires more knowledge about the religion of the other dialogue partners. Catholics must learn more about the religion of those with whom they live. . . . Moreover, Christians first of all should know their own faith before they begin to explore other world religions. The knowledge that Christians have of their faith has already slipped considerably in our secular societies. Are there ways to start a catechesis that would respond to the needs of our day and pursue both goals, namely, deepening one's own faith and also communicating one's knowledge of the faith convictions of others?

I would like to reaffirm your first statement. I am firmly convinced that there is no alternative to interreligious dialogue. The only alternatives would be tension and rivalry, alternatives that are not acceptable.

If this dialogue is to remain fruitful, a lot will be required of Catholics. First is knowledge: knowledge of their own religion, but also of the people with whom they live in a pluralistic society. Ignorant, completely secularized, indifferent Christians clearly are not equipped for interreligious dialogue in its various forms of development.

The first condition for interreligious dialogue is to love and live one's own faith. On this foundation is then built the solid knowledge of the other religion, which clarifies the similarities and the differences.

You ask about models for an appropriate catechesis. Already, there are many good beginnings. For example, the association of French-speaking Bishops Conferences of West Africa, which includes the bishops of nine countries, has an extremely effective commission for dialogue with Muslims. It has produced two working drafts that I would cite as an answer to your question. The first one gives recommendations for instructing Christians about Islam and the second one explains Christianity to Muslims. This second one helps Christians, for example, to explain their faith in a way that Muslims can understand. The first volume describes Islam in language and patterns that Christians can comprehend. This is only one example. Local commissions in many countries have have produced similar aids. I would recommend to Catholics that they study the *Catechism of the Catholic Church*. It is the best summary of our faith so far.

Even though the dialogue is relatively young, you have shown that it has borne positive fruits. But the weight of history still remains. Relics of earlier times, when there have been crusades, pogroms, holy wars, colonialism, battles between Muslim and Bahai or Hindu and Sikhs burden and still poison the dialogue between members of these faiths. To initiate interreligious dialogue don't we have to set aside all this historical baggage? Might that best happen when people begin to speak openly and stand ready to acknowledge fault and ask forgiveness? We saw an example of such a step when the Polish and German bishops acknowledged their need to deal with past oppression.

Such action would be praiseworthy, positive and very helpful. Indeed, the past can poison the present. Naturally we today are not responsible for things that happened some six hundred years ago. But today each of us lives in the continuity of our religious families that once were responsible on one side for crusades and on the other for holy wars. That means that we still carry the burden of history.

No one sees that more clearly than Pope John Paul II, who in preparation for the Holy Year expressed it openly in the great document *Tertio millennium adveniente*. He emphasizes this point repeatedly and summons the Church to a *mea culpa* for the guilt that Christians have incurred in the past — whether lay, clergy, bishops or even popes.

That does not mean that we should judge the past with the insights of the present, for we do not want to place ourselves in the pharisaical role of universal judges who highhandedly render opinions on everything that has happened in the last two thousand years. But objective research of the past can bring us to the point today at which we accept our responsibility and ask forgiveness.

Such a request for forgiveness is not a sign of weakness but rather of moral strength. If all religions were ready for such a *mea culpa* for their actions, it would certainly contribute toward peace in the world.

The greatest risk for the future of interreligous dialogue may not be the burden of history, but increased secularization, together with growing materialism and lack of interest in transcendence and religion. Such postmodern developments should give all faiths an even greater motivation for interreligious dialogue.

The phenomena you mention seem to me to pose a threat especially in the industrial societies of the West, precisely in proportion to their technological progress. With material success comes the temptation for people to consider God superfluous. In such an environment humankind can make itself the measure of all things. Then it is easy to claim moral acceptability for whatever is expedient.

In reality, many of industrialized societies have already become atheistic — but not motivated by any distinct anti-religious ideology or clearly formulated theory. I consider such societies more dangerous than ones that openly propagate atheism. Atheists at least speak of God, insofar as they make him the target of their ideological attacks; but materialistic, secular societies do not even mention his name. Lurking behind all this is the capital sin of pride. Undoubtedly, such developments threaten all religions. We should be aware of this when we meet for interreligious dialogue.

In light of such developments, it is not enough merely to exchange ideas about social justice, better distribution of goods and elimination of discrimination; we must address secular materialism as a real challenge for all religions.

On the other hand we notice a parallel tendency against increasing secularization. We see the rise of esoteric new forms of religion such as New Age. Is this "new syncretism" a response to today's interest in the media and virtual reality? How can the Church relate to such "pseudo-religions"?

We need to realize that behind these phenomena lies a search for religion, but it develops in a false direction and spawns bizarre developments. Behind it is a search for fulfillment and transcendence. That is why we should not dismiss such phenomena, but take them seriously.

We must look at ourselves for the causes and the deficiencies that have produced and encouraged such phenomena. We have to ask what people are really looking for when they go off into such cults. Where have we failed to answer such fundamental human questions as, What is ultimate truth? Where do I go for ultimate answers? Where have I come from and where am I going? These are the questions that Saint Augustine addressed in his famous dictum, "Our heart is restless until it rests in thee." Our first task is to help young people to find the way, as Saint Augustine did. As a young man he certainly went astray and made many mistakes. This is the great challenge that we face: helping people find God.

Let me conclude with a very broad question. Would you hazard a prognosis for the future of religion and interreligious dialogue?

I do not wish to play the prophet. Who am I to predict the future? But I pray and I hope. Therefore I am anything but pessimistic.

I pray for a future in which the adherents of different religions take each other seriously, relate openly to one another, respect one another, and recognize whatever truth they find in the religions of their dialogue partners, ready to learn from them whatever shows itself to be honorable and good. I hope for a future in which God becomes more and more the center of people's lives, in which the transcendent dimension of the human person stands out ever more clearly and in which a person's life no longer revolves around self but is open to his or her fellow human beings. I hope that this spirit will guide interreligious dialogue. I pray for a future in which Catholics know, love and live their faith better, so that they are prepared to share it with all those who will freely accept it.

Our goal is not one world religion, a mélange of different faiths. The goal is rather openness to the will of God. One prayer expresses my vision: "God, grant us your light, lead us in your ways. Help us to find your truth. Give us the courage to grasp and accept the truth and not to run away from it. Help us to know your Son Jesus Christ whom you have sent as the only savior for all humankind."

The Authors

Born in Nigeria in 1932 to parents who practiced an indigenous African religion, **Francis Arinze** converted to Christianity at the age of nine. He was ordained a priest in 1958, and was named bishop in 1965 and archbishop of Onitsha in 1967. In 1984, Pope John Paul II chose him to be president of the Vatican's Pontifical Council for Interreligious Dialogue, where he served until 2002. In 1985, Arinze was made a cardinal.

Cardinal Francis Arinze has been at the forefront of the Catholic Church's initiatives in interreligious relations for over 20 years. He has traveled the globe tirelessly, encouraging greater interfaith understanding.

Helmut S. Ruppert was born in Germany and has studied history, geography, and education. Since 1996, he has been the editor-in-chief of the German Catholic News Service.